PSALMS

Other Books by Martin G. Klingbeil

Seventh-day Adventist International
Bible Commentary, vol. 6—Psalms, chapters 1–75

PSALMS

Martin G. Klingbeil

Pacific Press®
Publishing Association
Nampa, Idaho | www.pacificpress.com

Cover design: Brandon Reese
Cover design resources: Lars Justinen

To order additional copies of this book or other Sabbath School companion books, call toll-free 1-800-765-6955, or visit Adventistbookcenter.com.

ISBN 978-0-8163-6889-1

July 2023

Dedication

To my family—Thandi, Jonathan, David,
and Matthias—whom I love deeply.

Contents

Preface

"The Lord is my Shepherd; I shall not want." These well-known words from Psalm 23:1 (KJV) were penned three thousand years ago by David, the shepherd turned king. They have been prayed in good times and bad, transcending religions, cultures, and languages. They are a message of divine provision and protection that speaks to the reality of human lives past and present. They provide insights into the personal piety of ancient believers, their walk with God, their joys and sorrows, questions and doubts, and even anguish and pain. All of this is embedded in a format of praise and prayer that can be recited and replicated again and again, speaking to the changing contexts of our lives and teaching us about God and His plan for us. Few other places in Scripture bring all of this together.

I want to invite the reader to take a journey with me through the book of Psalms, pausing and digging deeper, where need be, rejoicing with the joyful, weeping with the sad, and finally joining in with the universal choir that praises God in unison at the end of it all (Psalm 150). Along the way, there are stories to be told that illustrate how the psalms connect with our daily lives.

The book of Psalms was originally written in Hebrew, so I have divided each chapter—following a short introduction—into four sections that are entitled with Hebrew terms, reflecting the approach I am taking to the study of Psalms.

Davar. The Hebrew term *davar* means "word"—in this context, God's Word. In most cases, this part is the longest section of the chapter because I want to give prominence to the biblical text in its context, focusing on an in-depth study of specific psalms that relate to the chapter's main topic. "In God, whose word I praise, in God I trust; I shall not be afraid. What can flesh do to me?" (Psalm 56:4, ESV).

Pesher. An Aramaic word that is often found in the Aramaic section of the book of Daniel, *pesher* means "interpretation." In Daniel 5:26, it is used to describe God's prophet interpreting the writing on the wall to King Belshazzar. The section focuses on the theological interpretation of the chapter topic, trying to look at the bigger picture. Aramaic is closely related to Hebrew, and the word also occurs in the Hebrew text of Ecclesiastes: "Who is like a wise man? And who knows the interpretation of a thing?" (Ecclesiastes 8:1).

Edut. The Hebrew word *edut* means "testimony," and this section of the chapter will offer ways to connect the psalms with our daily lives. We all have a story to tell and a testimony to give. "Your testimonies are my delight; they are my counselors" (Psalm 119:24, ESV).

Tehillim. The Hebrew word *tehillim* means "praises" and also happens to be the original name of the book of Psalms. The *tehillim* section invites one to end each chapter with praise and/or prayer. There are a variety of hymns, contextualized paraphrases of psalms, poetic renditions of psalms, and a bit of personal poetry from my side. "Praise the Lord! Sing to the LORD a new song, his praise in the assembly of the godly!" (Psalm 149:1, ESV).

At the end of this book, I hope you can join me in a prayer of praise and affirmation to God. "Yes, You are my Shepherd—You are all that I want."

1

How to Read the Psalms

The psalms are poetry, Hebrew poetry. Most English versions of the Bible indicate poetry through alternating lines of indented text, in contrast to prose's justified text. This difference between prose and poetry is apparent when, for example, the book of Psalms is compared with the book of Genesis. However, poetic lines can also be inserted into narrative contexts, and the first example of this is in Genesis 2:23 when Adam reacts to Eve's beauty, naming her "woman." I can sympathize with Adam's poetic moment as I recall writing a poem for my future wife when we got engaged—not in Hebrew, but in German.

Nevertheless, Hebrew poetry works differently than modern Western poetry. Often, we understand poetry as a way of expressing something in a roundabout way or in a more ornate fashion, an aesthetic expression of what could have been said more plainly. Hebrew poetry, on the other hand, is employed when theologically significant content, often divine speech (see Genesis 3:14–16), needs to be communicated. It tends to be shorter and more compact than prose, often implying syntactic elements from previous lines (e.g., verbal ellipsis).

Hebrew poetry seems to be more capable of painting complex pictures.

Psalms

An example of this is Judges 4 and 5, which tells a story, first in prose (Judges 4), and then in poetry (Judges 5). It is the courageous and gruesome killing of Sisera, a commander in the army of Jabin, the Canaanite king of Hazor, by Jael, the wife of Heber the Kenite. The story climaxes when Sisera, on the run after the Canaanite army has been defeated by Barak, seeks to hide in Jael's tent because her husband is an ally of the king of Hazor. Jael skillfully lures him into a false sense of security before she murders him:

And he said to her, "Please, pour me a little bit of water because I am thirsty." So she opened a skin bottle of milk and gave him a drink; then she covered him (Judges 4:19, author's translation).

For water he asked;
Milk she gave;
In a bowl fit for lords,
She brought creamed yogurt
(Judges 5:25, author's translation).

In the Hebrew text of Judges 4:19, there are fourteen words in prose, but there are only eight words in the corresponding poetic text of Judges 5:25. The prose describes a sequence of events in the storyline as Jael attends to Sisera when he enters her tent: from a "little bit of water" to a "skin bottle of milk" and eventually to a blanket as she "covered him." The poetic version of the same moment in the story works with parallel and simultaneous contrasts, juxtaposing "water" and "milk" with each other at the beginning of two consecutive lines before the two verbs "ask" and "give." Sisera asks little, but Jael gives much more than Sisera expects. The third and fourth lines zoom in on the initial contrast by characterizing the bowl as a special vessel designed for nobility and the milk as curdled, most probably a type of rich, creamy yogurt that is fit for kings. Furthermore, the Hebrew verb *qarab*, meaning "to bring," is often found in religious contexts (see Leviticus 10:19), which characterizes Jael's attention to Sisera in terms of a ritual of homage reserved for human dignitaries or even God. The poetic version of the story is a slightly different and more subtle form

12

of the tale, using fewer words but more emotive details.

Thus, the Psalms, as a fully poetic book, provides us with important insights into the inner workings of the psalmists' minds and emotions as they experienced God in daily life. This feature makes the psalms accessible and relatable, even after millennia have passed since they were penned.[1]

Davar—Reading the psalms

Becoming acquainted with some of the main characteristics of Hebrew poetry can be helpful in reading and understanding the book of Psalms. While it is not always possible to preserve the intricate nuances of the original Hebrew text (like the assonance of *mishpat* and *mishpakh* in Isaiah 5:7 that sounds very similar in contrast to the corresponding English "justice" and "bloodshed"), modern versions are increasingly sensitive to the features of Hebrew poetry and try to capture them through their translations.

The ancient manuscripts of the Old Testament differentiated between prose and poetry by breaking the text into poetic lines (called *colon* in the singular, *cola* in the plural) and adding divisional markers. Besides this visual distinction (called *colography*), the most fundamental characteristic of Hebrew poetry is the parallelism between consecutive lines. Unlike modern Western poetry, which is characterized by rhyme and meter,[2] Hebrew poetry creates a correspondence between lines that follow each other. This correspondence can take place in a number of different ways and was first defined in 1753 by the Anglican bishop Robert Lowth, who originally differentiated between three categories of parallelism in Hebrew poetry:[3]

1. *Synonymous parallelism* occurs when a second line provides a synonymous restatement of the first line.

Praise the LORD, all you Gentiles!

Laud Him, all you peoples! (Psalm 117:1).

2. *Antithetical parallelism* places the second line in opposition to the first.

A wise son makes a glad father,
But a foolish son is the grief of his mother (Proverbs 10:1).

3. *Synthetic parallelism* has the second line complete, complement, or expand on the first line.

He brought me to the banqueting house,
And his banner over me was love (Song of Solomon 2:4).

However, parallelism should not be confused with reiteration or redundancy, as the parallel lines often enhance, modify, or intensify the first through the second line. A "glad father" in Proverbs 10:1 is contrasted with a grieving mother, which clearly intensifies the negative emotional impact that a wise versus a foolish son has on his parents.

Beyond the initial categories developed by Lowth, students of Hebrew poetry realized that correspondence could also occur on other levels that can be found in consecutive lines.

4. *Word pairs* are terms that are often used together and follow each other in consecutive lines or are in close proximity to each other.

Whom have I in heaven but You?
And there is none upon earth that I desire besides You (Psalm 73:25).

The word pair *heaven-earth* in Psalm 73:25, occurring throughout the Old Testament (cf. Genesis 1:1), does not refer to two different domains but constitutes a description of the totality of the created world or cosmos and the psalmist's desire for God, no matter where he finds himself in history and in the world.

5. *Grammatical parallelism* is a grammatical correspondence or contrast between lines.

> For in death there is no remembrance of You;
> In the grave who will give You thanks? (Psalm 6:5).

A statement in the first line is paralleled with a rhetorical question in the second line, underlining our need to connect with God while we are alive.

6. *Semantic parallelism* is the association of words that belong to the same categories of meaning.

> He has declared to His people the power of His works,
> In giving them the heritage of the nations (Psalm 111:6).

"His people" and "the nations" belong to the same category of meaning: the semantic domain of *groups and classes of people*. At the same time, there is a progression from God's people to the nations as the blessings of divinely elected Israel also extend to the other nations.

7. *Phonetic parallelism* presents similar-sounding words or parts of words.

> The Lord, the LORD Almighty, has a day
> of tumult and trampling and terror (Isaiah 22:5, NIV).

This is a difficult one to replicate in translation, but the New International Version has made an excellent attempt at reproducing the alliterations and duplications between the Hebrew *mehumah—mebusah—mebukah* in translating them as "tumult"—"trampling"—"terror."

8. *Chiasm* is a term drawn from the Greek letter *chi* (X). A chiasm creates a concentric steplike structure with correspondence between poetic lines as they move toward and away from a midpoint (e.g., A-B-B'-A' or A-B-C-B'-A').

A In days of old (God's past deeds)
   B You drove out the nations (past victories)
      C Nor did their arm save them (victory not by human strength)
         D Your right hand (victory by divine intervention)
            E You are my King, O God (trust in God as King)
         D' Through Your name (victory by divine intervention)
      C' Nor shall my sword save me (victory not by human strength)
   B' You have saved us from our enemies (past victories)
A' Praise Your name forever (praise to God in the present) (Psalm 44:1–8).

It is interesting to note that the Hebrew name for God (*'elohim*) can be found at the beginning, the center, and the end, communicating the important central message of the passage—that trust in God as our King in the present is rooted in His past and future acts.

Inclusio refers to a correspondence between the beginning and ending lines of psalms or passages.

> I was glad when they said to me,
> "Let us go into the house of the LORD."
> . . .
> Because of the house of the LORD our God
> I will seek your good (Psalm 122:1–9).

The "house of the Lord"—the temple—creates a frame around the psalm, creating a thematic focus on the peace of Jerusalem as being dependent on God's presence in the city.

Beyond the parallelism of poetic lines, there are other poetic elements that effectively communicate the message of the psalmists.

Key words are significant words or combinations of words that are related to each other in the original Hebrew. In Psalm 122, "peace" (Hebrew *shalom*) occurs three times (verses 6, 7, 8) and "Jerusalem" (Hebrew *yerushalaim*) three times as well (verses 2, 3, 6). Both words are related in Hebrew and once more strengthen the message that peace in Jerusalem, the "city of peace," can only come from the sanctuary.

Acrostics structure a poem so that each sequential line or stanza begins with the next letter of the Hebrew alphabet. The longest psalm, Psalm 119, consists of 176 verses, divided into 22 stanzas with eight lines or verses in each stanza. The lines in each stanza begin with the same letter of the Hebrew alphabet, followed by the next stanza, whose eight verses all begin with the next letter of the Hebrew alphabet. Acrostic poems were easier to memorize, and beyond Psalm 119, there are a number of other acrostics in the Psalter (Psalms 9; 10; 25; 34; 37; 111; 112; 145).

All of these literary devices demonstrate the skillful artistry of the authors and work hand in hand with divine inspiration to transmit the theological message of the Psalms.

Pesher—Doxology unlocks theology

The book of Psalms is a book of praise, and its Hebrew title *tehillim*, or "praises," captures what the Psalter is all about, that is, to praise God. It would seem that what we know about God (theology) would lead us to praise Him (doxology); however, the subtitle above has reversed the direction: as we praise God, we get to know Him. Even more, our praise clears the way for us to know Him better. Through the psalms, God is teaching us that doxology unlocks theology.

The God we learn about in the Psalms is a personal God whose presence (and, sometimes, perceived absence) is keenly experienced by the psalmist

(Psalms 23:4; 27:9; 42:1, 2). He is a God who is actively involved in the life of His children, from Creation (Psalm 115:15, 16), through the Exodus, the conquest of the Promised Land, and the turbulent time of the united and divided monarchies (Psalms 77; 78; 105; 106; 135; 136). God's kingship provides the paradigm for Israelite kingship (Psalms 2; 20; 45; 72; 110) as He reigns from the sanctuary, which in the Psalms can reference both the temple in Jerusalem and also the heavenly sanctuary (Psalms 20:2, 6; 50:2; 99:1, 2; 135:21; 150:1). God as a just Judge (Psalms 96:13; 97:2) vindicates His people (Psalm 35:27) and takes care of the socially marginalized (Psalm 146:5–10). His mercy and forgiveness (Psalm 103:8) invite a response of praise and worship from Israel, His elected people (Psalm 117).

Thus, praise holds the book of Psalms together and permeates it, with each of the five sections climaxing in a doxology (Psalm 41:13; 72:18, 19; 89:52; 106:48; 150). The Psalms present a theological cross section of the Old Testament with an ever-present prophetic and messianic perspective that finds its antitypical counterpart in the life, death, and resurrection of Jesus of Nazareth, the Christ (see Psalm 22).[4]

Edut—Seeing the psalms

A picture is worth a thousand words, and the book of Psalms is full of imagery that helps us to see the psalms[5] and, more precisely, the God of the psalms. Metaphors give us insights into the character of God in a way that theological reflection rarely achieves. They open a window through which we can see who God is and how He deals with humanity.

Maybe God chose to reveal Himself to the psalmists by way of analogy so that our finite human mind has a chance to grasp the infinite: "A metaphor helps us to understand an unknown reality (God) by means of a more familiar reality (e.g., the shepherd), and it is interesting how our theological thinking (our thinking about God) is largely informed by these metaphors."[6]

There are more than five hundred occurrences of metaphors for God in the book of Psalms (for more details, see chapter 3), demonstrating how frequently the psalmists resorted to the language of imagery when they spoke to and about God. The divine *Shepherd* (Psalm 23:1–4) is still providing and leading, even in the darkest valleys; the *royal host* (verses 5, 6) treats us lavishly with a banquet table, foreshadowing another banquet with a divine *host* when earth's history comes to a close (Revelation 19:6–9); God as a *Father* (Psalm 89:26) takes care of the orphans and the widows (Psalm 68:5); He is a *Rock* to which I can flee (Psalm 18:2), providing me with the strength that I lack; a mighty *fortress* where I am safe (Psalm 46:7); an invincible *warrior* who fights my battles (Psalm 68:7–27); He is my *Light* (Psalm 27:1) illuminating my darkest moments; and again and again there is God's *face* that shines upon me (Psalm 67:1) and His *hand* that holds me and leads me on (Psalm 139:10).[7] When reading these images in Psalms, I can almost see Him.

Tehillim—An Old English acrostic on Psalm 117

P raise him that ay

R emaines the same:

A ll tongues display

I ehovas fame.

S ing all that share

T his earthly ball:

H is mercies are

E xpos'd to all:

L ike as the word

O nce he doth give,

R old in record,

D oth tyme outlive.

       —Mary Sidney, Countess of Pembroke, *Laudate Dominum*[8]

1. See Martin G. Klingbeil, "Introduction to Hebrew Poetry and Wisdom Books," in *Andrews Bible Commentary: Light. Depth. Truth*, ed. Ángel Manuel Rodríguez (Berrien Springs, MI: Andrews University Press, 2020), 1:614–623.

2. Hebrew poetry nevertheless creates rhythm through parallelism as each *colon* usually consists of three words and each poetic line has two to four *cola*.

3. "The correspondence of one verse or line with another, I call parallelism." Robert Lowth, *Isaiah: A New Translation; With a Preliminary Dissertation, and Notes, Critical, Philological, and Explanatory* (London: J. Dodsley and T. Cadelle, 1788), 6, https://www.retoricabiblicaesemitica.org/wp-content/uploads/2019/03/lowth3_isaiah-1.pdf.

4. Dragoslava Santrac, "Theology of Psalms," in *Seventh-day Adventist International Bible Commentary*, ed. Jacques Doukhan, vol. 6, *Psalms, Proverbs, Ecclesiastes, Song of Songs* (Nampa, ID: Pacific Press®, 2022), 22–36.

5. See the helpful book by William P. Brown, *Seeing the Psalms: A Theology of Metaphor* (Louisville, KY: Westminster John Knox Press, 2002).

6. Martin G. Klingbeil, "Psalms 1–75," in Doukhan, *Seventh-day Adventist International Bible Commentary*, 6:21.

7. God's face (46 times) and His hand (54 times) are by far the most frequently used metaphors of the divine used in Psalms.

8. The acrostic was written sometime between 1593 and 1600 and summarizes the last line of the shortest psalm in the psalter, Psalm 117. J. C. A. Rathmell, *The Psalms of Sir Philip Sidney and the Countess of Pembroke* (Garden City, NY: Anchor Books, 1963), 272.

2

Teach Us to Pray

Aside from the Lord's Prayer (Matthew 6:9–13), Psalm 23 is one of the most widely recited prayers in the history of Christianity. It has influenced the liturgies of churches and has been prayed by soldiers in dark trenches and recalled from fading memories in the last hours of a long life.[1] Psalm 23, known as the Shepherd psalm, is full of ancient imagery that can still be relevant in modern life.

It was a rather hot July day in 1998 at Tall al-'Umayri in the beautiful country of Jordan. I had joined an archaeological expedition—my first one—conducted by the Madaba Plains Project, and sponsored by Andrews University and La Sierra University. Together with a group of Polish archaeologists, I was excavating the area around a dolmen tomb, which had been discovered during the 1994 excavation season. These "tombs are impressive house-like structures built of large stone slabs that stand on bedrock."[2] They usually consist of upright standing slabs that are capped with a horizontal slab marking the entrance to a burial cave. In the western hemisphere, there are dolmens at the famous site of Stonehenge in England that are at least six thousand years old. Similarly, the dolmen tomb at Tall al-'Umayri is dated to the Early Bronze Age IB around 3100 BC. In ancient and even into modern times, it has been a place where the living buried and remembered their dead, where feasts were celebrated, and where communities met. Interestingly, the dolmen tomb seems to have existed even before people settled permanently at the site (cf. Genesis 23).

But back to the hot July day. Since the tomb was located on the southeastern lower slope of the tell,[3] it was regrettably protected from a cooling breeze that usually blew across the top of the site from a westerly direction. It was also mercilessly exposed to the summer sun, which made any short interruption to the arduous excavation work most welcome.

The interruption came in the form of bleating sheep a short distance away. I was vigorously working on an interesting layer of soil that looked like it could be a plastered surface adjacent to the dolmen when I heard someone shout, "*Yalla, Yalla,*" Arabic for "let's go, hurry up." I looked up, thankful for the opportunity to straighten my back and have a short break from the dust, and there he was: the shepherd! It appeared that he had stepped right out of Psalm 23 as he slowly led his flock through a small valley separating the tell from an adjacent hill.

I scrambled for my camera as I watched him directing the flock with just the tone of his voice, a staff in his hands, and a keffiyeh (Arab checkered black and white scarf) around his head. I had observed shepherds with their flocks in other countries, herding their animals in front of them with the help of sheepdogs, and had always wondered how the biblical shepherd had done it. How did he lead his flock to greener pastures and sweeter waters? And how did he guide them with just the tone of his voice through the valleys of shadows of death (John 10:4, 5)? As I watched the shepherd slowly move out of sight, I thought once more of the width and depth of the prayer in Psalm 23. In just six brief verses, it includes good and bad times, feasts and fears, provisions and protections, and, ultimately, a deep glimpse into the abundant mercy of the divine Shepherd.

Davar—The Lord is my Shepherd

Psalm 23:1 consists of four short words in Hebrew that are translated into nine English words, demonstrating once more that a lot can be said in Hebrew poetry with only a few words:[4] "The Lord is my Shepherd; I shall not want." David, king of Israel and former shepherd, sets the record straight right at the outset that it is the Lord, the divine Shepherd, who is leading the king. The ultimate authority belongs to God, and He is the One who directs our paths, but not from a detached distance: to David, Yahweh is "my" shepherd, pointing to a very intimate relationship between the Israelite king and his divine Shepherd who leads him through the green pastures and also through the dark valleys of life.

The second part of Psalm 23:1 is syntactically arranged as a consequence of the first part: the Lord is my Shepherd, therefore "I shall not want" (literally: "I do not lack"). The sentence is missing a direct object, thus illustrating the point that God takes care of all our needs—not necessarily of all our wants, though. In a modern world of instant gratification, His provisions may not always correspond to what we think we need or when we need it, but to what the Shepherd considers necessary to sustain our life with His abundance.

Psalm 23:2, 3 unpack what the Shepherd does to provide for His sheep, and there are three expressions that appear to allude to the daily tasks of a real shepherd in ancient Israel, or Jordan for that matter: the shepherd leads his flock to grassy pastures (literally: "dwellings of grass") to feed his flock, he searches for still waters (literally: "waters of rest"), and he leads them along straight paths (literally: "tracks of righteousness"). A rich imagery of overabundance and perfect provision is created, making me think that I would rather be a sheep. No worries, no cares, just green grass, clear water, and straight paths. However, David chooses his words carefully to make sure that nobody is tempted to think of this tranquil bliss only in terms of material blessings. He uses words that have strong theological implications throughout the Old Testament: there is "rest" ("waters of rest"), which elsewhere refers to the rest that God promised His people on the threshold to the Promised Land (Deuteronomy 12:9) or rest as peace through God's protection from war (1 Kings 8:56).

We can think beyond the Old Testament to the repose that is promised in Hebrews 4 as the ultimate rest in connection with the Sabbath rest. The idea is clear: humankind rests, and God acts. We could also call this righteousness by faith and not by works. Next, "righteousness" ("tracks of righteousness") is actually mentioned, a theological key word throughout the Old Testament. It is an expression of God's character (Psalm 7:17) and the criterium for His judgments (Psalm 35:24). All of this serves to restore our lives. The Hebrew word translated as "restore" actually means "make return" or "to bring back." Another form of the same word is used throughout the Old Testament as the technical term for repentance (1 Kings 8:33). God restores us and brings the wayward sheep back into the fold and into His loving arms.

This shows us that Psalm 23 is more than a song about happy sheep, and, after verse 3, there are actually no more happy sheep. Psalm 23:4 serves as a turning point in the psalm, and it changes the tune in a number of ways.

First, happiness and abundance are replaced by life-threatening darkness, and the Hebrew uses a superlative expression here ("valley of deathly darkness"). While sheep in ancient Israel certainly had to be herded through dark gorges and canyons after leaving the grassy pastures in order to get home, again, the choice of words seems to point beyond the basic sheepish dimension to the spiritual experience. The dark and deathly valleys of our lives are as much a reality as are the sunny meadows and refreshing waters. Even if the shepherd in the impenetrable darkness is not visible anymore, David assures us that He is still there, right beside us.

Another interesting change that occurs in verse 4 is a change from third to second person. David is now talking directly to the divine Shepherd, and the death-valley experience turns into a powerful personal experience with his God. After all, the death valleys of our lives are often exactly the places that give us the most intimate glimpses and understanding of God's love.

Finally, verse 4 introduces a third important change: the shepherd imagery gradually makes way for the image of God as the royal host. It does so by mentioning the rod and the staff as the means by which the psalmist is comforted. The rod literally refers to a short scepter, the insignia of a king, whereas the staff is the longer shepherd's staff with which he provides support for the sheep. The scepter (rod) serves to break up the nations (Psalm 2:9) or to punish (cf. Psalm 2:9; Isaiah 10:5), and the staff is a means of support (Zechariah 8:4). One of the church fathers, Cassiodorus (AD 490–585) provides an interesting perspective on the rod and staff: "The 'rod' denotes the justice and strength of the Lord Savior. . . . 'Staff' indicates the support he provides for us."[5] In that way, justice (rod) and mercy (staff) meet each other in the hands of our Shepherd and King, who is the only one that can bring them together.

Pesher—Not just my Shepherd, but also my King

While shepherds and kings are not necessarily associated in our modern mind, in ancient Israel and beyond, they were: David was a shepherd and became king. Even other ancient Near Eastern kings, like Hammurabi, the king of ancient Babylon (reigned 1792–1750 BC), referred to themselves as "the shepherd of the oppressed."[6] The last three verses blend the metaphor of God as Shepherd with that of God as King, and more specifically, describe God as a royal host, thus moving the psalm to its grand theological finale.

While the shepherd in Psalm 23:2, 3 did three things to provide for his sheep, the royal host in verse 5 does three things to make his guest feel truly welcome. First, He prepares a table, which is the kingly thing to do (2 Samuel 9:7–13), but this royal banquet is set right in the face of the psalmist's enemies. It is important to understand that the rules of ancient Near Eastern hospitality dictate that a guest who resides under one's roof cannot be touched by an enemy. He is under the protection of the host, who will do anything in his power to protect his guests. This role is seen in the story of Lot and the angels who visited him in Sodom (Genesis 19): he desperately offers his daughters to the mob outside in order to protect his guests. But in Psalm 23, God is the host, and His guests can sit down in perfect peace even in the face of their enemies. Eating is a rather defenseless act, and the fascinating story of Elisha and the blindness-struck Syrian soldiers demonstrates how a banquet may even turn enemies into friends (2 Kings 6:8–23).

The royal treatment goes on, and oil is poured onto the guest's head, a ritual reserved only for those invited by the king (Luke 7:46). The aromatic smell elevates and has healing properties, allowing God's guests to relax and feel special in the house of the Lord. Then there is a cup that overflows and satisfies all possible thirst (John 4:14). Ancient Near Eastern hospitality, in contrast with Western etiquette, dictates that an empty cup needs to be refilled until the guest does not empty it anymore.

Psalm 23:6 provides a hint as to the contents of the bottomless cup: goodness and mercy. As the shepherd image moved beyond the material needs of the sheep to our spiritual needs, the image of the royal host also moved. There is mention of mercy (Hebrew *khesed*, meaning "loving-kindness, goodness, grace, mercy"),[7] and while *righteousness* was the theological key word in the Shepherd image ("paths of righteousness"), it is now *mercy*, which points to the theological dimension of the image of God as a royal host. As guests in God's house, we will be followed by (literally, "pursued") mercy, and consequently, we will always want to return to the house of the Lord. As the metaphors of God as a Shepherd and as King blend perfectly in this psalm, the powerful message of David's prayer in Psalm 23 is the perfect blending of justice and mercy in our Shepherd and King as He leads, provides, comforts, protects, and, ultimately, redeems.

Edut—Meditate

Every prayer that recites Psalm 23 invokes these qualities of God as Shepherd and King, applying them to the widely varying circumstances of life that call for prayer. As a matter of fact, in times of trouble, the Bible's authors often used Scripture to pray their most urgent prayers. For example, at least fourteen different psalms are alluded to in Jonah's prayer from the belly of the fish (Jonah 2), psalms that he must have committed to memory long before his journey away from Nineveh (cf. 2 Samuel 22; Isaiah 38; Habakkuk 3; Daniel 2:20–23; etc.).[8]

Psalm 1 begins with a description of the righteous and exalts him as one who continuously meditates on *torah* (Psalm 1:2), referring to the totality of God's instruction through His Word. While our ideas of "meditation" are often influenced by Far Eastern practices of self-centering or self-emptying, the Hebrew verb *hagah*, meaning "meditate, moan, speak," in contrast, refers to "a continuous soft 'uttering' of God's Word"[9]—a quiet but audible recitation of Scripture.

Yes, "prayer is the opening of the heart to God as to a friend,"[10] and our prayers do not need to use prescribed or ceremonial language in order to reach the throne room of the Almighty. Reciting Scripture in prayer appropriates and applies its inspired messages to our current situations and claims the divine promises embedded in its sacred pages.

Tehillim—Psalm 23

GOD, my shepherd!
    I don't need a thing.
You have bedded me down in lush meadows,
    you find me quiet pools to drink from.
True to your word,
    you let me catch my breath
    and send me in the right direction.

Even when the way goes through
   Death Valley,
I'm not afraid
   when you walk at my side.
Your trusty shepherd's crook
   makes me feel secure.

You serve me a six-course dinner
   right in front of my enemies.
You revive my drooping head;
   my cup brims with blessing.

Your beauty and love chase after me
   every day of my life.
I'm back home in the house of GOD
   for the rest of my life (*The Message*).

---

1. William L. Holladay, *The Psalms Through Three Thousand Years: Prayerbook of a Cloud of Witnesses* (Minneapolis, MN: Fortress, 1993), 6–14.

2. Gloria London, "A Ceremonial Center for the Living and the Dead," *Near Eastern Archaeology* 74, no. 4 (2011): 216–225.

3. A tell (Hebrew) or tall (Arabic) is an artificial mound or hill that has been created through the accumulation of successive ancient settlements built on top of each other.

4. Martin G. Klingbeil, "Introduction to Hebrew Poetry and Wisdom Books," in *Andrews Bible Commentary: Light. Depth. Truth.*, ed. Ángel Manuel Rodríguez (Berrien Springs, MI: Andrews University Press, 2020), 1:614–623.

5. Quentin F. Wesselschmidt, ed., *Psalms 51–150*, vol. 8, *Ancient Christian Commentary on Scripture, Old Testament* (Downers Grove, IL: InterVarsity, 2007), 180.

6. Martin G. Klingbeil, "Psalms 1-75," in *Seventh-day Adventist International Bible Commentary*, ed. Jacques Doukhan, vol. 6, *Psalms, Proverbs, Ecclesiastes, Song of Songs* (Nampa, ID: Pacific Press®, 2022), 122.

7. *Khesed* is "the essence of *YHWH* as the God of the covenant (cf. 1 Kgs 8:23)." Klingbeil, "Psalms 1–75," 125.

8. James W. Watts, "Biblical Psalms Outside the Psalter," in *The Book of Psalms: Com-*

position and Reception, ed. Peter W. Flint and Patrick D. Miller, Supplements to *Vetus Testamentum*, vol. 99 (Leiden and Boston: Brill, 2005), 288–309.

9. Klingbeil, "Psalms 1–75," 45.

10. Ellen G. White, *Steps to Christ* (Washington, DC: Review and Herald®, 1956), 93.

3

The Lord Reigns

The deities of the ancient Near East come in all shapes and sizes. Images of the divine abounded among ancient Israel's polytheistic neighbors and are characterized in the text of the Old Testament as a constant threat to Israel's monotheistic religion (Exodus 20:3; Deuteronomy 6:4). Additionally, Israel's religion was aniconic, based on the commandment prohibiting graven images (Exodus 20:4–6). Throughout the history of the Old Testament, there were repeated religious reforms that were intended to reform Israel by destroying pagan idols (e.g., 2 Kings 18:4).[1] These reforms were initiated by the prophets of the Old Testament who fought against the threat of idolatry (Amos 5:26; Hosea 9:10; Isaiah 46:1; Jeremiah 25:6; Ezekiel 8:14), a spiritual hazard that began during the conquest of Canaan when Israel was unable or unwilling to remove the pagan deities from the land (Joshua 23:7–16; 24:15; 2 Kings 17:5–17).

The Bible mentions a number of foreign gods that were worshiped throughout the lands of the Bible.[2] There is Asherah, the Canaanite mother-goddess (1 Kings 18:19), whose name can also refer to a treelike cultic object (Deuteronomy 16:21). Baal is probably the most frequently mentioned foreign god in the Old Testament (ca. ninety times) and refers to the Canaanite storm-god, also known as Baal-Hadad, often brandishing a lightning spear in one hand and a club raised above his head in the other hand, representing the thunderclap (see figure 1). He is usually depicted as standing upon the mountains, the secure abode of the Canaanite pantheon. The references to Baal in the Old Testament are usually negative in character and attest to the problem of syncretism.

This issue even elicited a response in poetry: Psalm 29 appears to be modeled on a Canaanite hymn to the weather- and storm-god Baal but "rather serves as a well-aimed polemic against Canaanite mythology, demonstrating the monotheistic supremacy of *YHWH* over all the gods of Canaan."[3] The seven thunderclaps of the "voice of the Lord" (Psalm 29:3–9) demonstrate God's

Figure 1. "Baal au foudre" stela (Louvre, Paris)

superiority as even the mountains "skip . . . like a young wild ox" (verse 6). "Sirion" in this verse is the Canaanite name for Mount Hermon, a clear literary attack against Canaanite religion, which sees the mountains as the unmovable abode of the gods and especially of Baal.

Then there are Adrammelech (2 Kings 17:31), Ashtoreth (1 Kings 11:5), Bel (Jeremiah 51:44), Chemosh (1 Kings 11:7), Dagon (1 Samuel 5:2), Merodach/Marduk (Jeremiah 50:2), Milcom (1 Kings 11:5), Molech (Leviticus 20:2), Nebo (Isaiah 46:1), Nergal (2 Kings 17:30), Nisroch (Isaiah 37:38), Tammuz (Ezekiel 8:14)—the list goes on and on. The process of fabricating these gods in the form of wooden idols is detailed in Scripture, pointing to the absurdity of humans fabricating their own gods from a part of the same piece of wood that they burn to keep themselves warm (Isaiah 44:9–20).

The fabrication of idols is a result of the age-old human tendency to make gods for themselves, creating them in their own image, leaving humankind with worthless gods who—like their worshipers—engage in epic and bloody battles with each other, act capriciously when bothered by humans, and wait grudgingly to be appeased by human sacrifices.

Davar—Creator, King, and Judge

Maybe we should let God speak for Himself instead of making Him in our own image. The book of Psalms is full of metaphors by which God has revealed Himself, helping us to understand Him. These representations respond to the human need for illustration, helping us see the Unseeable by way of analogy. Scholars have observed that "all, or almost all, of the language used by the Bible to refer to God is metaphor,"[4] pointing to the fact that imagery often communicates better than words.

A survey of metaphors of God in the book of Psalms reveals over five hundred instances of metaphorical speech about God in the book of Psalms, which can be divided into seventeen main categories of metaphor.

We will highlight three metaphors for God that appear frequently in the Psalms. They speak to a crucial understanding of who God is and how He relates to His creatures. The metaphors of God as *Creator, King,* and *Judge* relate to the past, present, and future; our origins, our current relationship with God, and our final destiny.

God as *Creator* (Genesis 1) does not seem to be a metaphor because this is what God is from the beginning of Scripture. However, in the book of Psalms, "creation motifs are utilized to highlight numerous aspects of divine activity, such as the election of Israel, the Exodus, the deliverance of the psalmist from trouble, and God's ongoing providence and preservation of His creation."[5] Thus, the creative power of God builds on but goes beyond the historical event of Creation and continues to be metaphorically applied to such important events as the Exodus (Psalms 136; 78, the creation of Israel as a people [Psalm 95]), and even the creative knitting together of each individual in their mother's womb (Psalm 139).

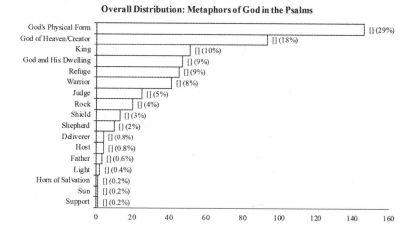

Overall Distribution: Metaphors of God in the Psalms

Beyond these metaphorical creative events, there is the sustenance of creation that describes God in creation language. Psalm 65 is particularly rich in describing God as *Creator* in the provision of rain and fertility on the land. After a praise in the sanctuary (Psalm 65:1–4) that establishes an interesting link between creation, God's provisions, and the Day of Atonement (Leviticus 16), a description of God as *Creator* in general (Psalm 65:5–8), and His provisions for the land of Israel in particular (Psalm 65:9–13) follows. Ultimately, God's provisions are aimed at atonement, for all that He does from Creation to re-creation serves the purpose of reconciling us with Him.[6]

When I ask my students whether God is *King*, the "yes" and "no" answers tend to balance each other out. While God is the King of kings (Revelation 17:14), He is so not like human kings who conquer other nations and exploit their subjects. That is the power of metaphor, as it compares the Infinite (God) with something finite (king), and the possibilities and limitations of the comparison (e.g., while God is worthy to be served, He does not exact our service) create new meanings and even new understandings of human kingship. Israelite kings were supposed to model their kingship on the ideal paradigm of God as *King* and not on the kings of the surrounding nations. When Israel asks Samuel to give them a king like all the other nations (1 Samuel 8:5), God instructs Samuel to paint them a dire picture of human kingship with all its extortions and exploitations (verses 10–18). Moses had already foreseen this moment and, under inspiration, had delimited the rights and duties of a king (Deuteronomy 17:14–20).

Psalm 72 is a beautiful prayer of King David, offered shortly before his death, as he had made Solomon, his son, co-regent (cf. 1 Kings 1). His prayer provided a paradigm for Solomon's reign: he "will judge [God's] people with righteousness" (Psalm 72:2), bring "justice to the poor" (verses 4, 2), provide abundance and stability to the land (verses 5, 6), and the "righteous shall flourish" (verse 7) during his reign. Thus, God would extend the king's dominion (verses 8–11) because he is taking care of the "needy" and the "poor" (verses 4, 12). Verses 12–14 are dedicated to the king's effort to avert the plight of the poor. This extends not only his territory but also his longevity so that his subjects will bless him as he is a blessing to them (verses 15–17).

The prayer needs to be read against the backdrop of the so-called royal psalms (Psalms 93; 96–99), which describe God in His majesty as a king who is worthy of our service and praise. He is our protector and provider; He elevates us, sustains our daily life, and is worthy of our worship and service. He rules in our hearts and sits enthroned in our minds—life under His rule is good. The dreadful alternative is to serve the "ruler of this world" (John 12:31), who is the "god of this age" (2 Corinthians 4:4)—Satan.

God as *Judge* is possibly one of the more uncomfortable images of God, especially from the perspective of a modern Western worldview. How often do we hurl a "Don't judge me!" at each other to avoid any form of (at times even justified) criticism or accountability? Accordingly, our image of God as a *Judge* is assuming a stern deity who is just waiting for us to step out of line in order to mete out a just but harsh punishment. Popular culture does not like the God of the Old Testament as *Judge*.[7]

The psalmist understood the Divine Judge differently, and Psalm 7 sheds some light on God as *Judge*: the psalmist appeals to God as a "just judge" (verse 11) who will judge "according to [the psalmist's] integrity" (verse 8). This is not self-righteous impunity but a righteousness that is based on God's "righteousness" (verses 9, 17). He is the psalmist's "defense" (verse 10) and vindicates the widows (Psalm 68:5), the oppressed (Psalm 76:9), and the poor (Psalm 72:2).

Pesher—Assurance of salvation

C. S. Lewis notes the difference between the psalmist's and the Christian's image of God as *Judge*: "The ancient Jews, like ourselves, think of God's judgment in terms of an earthly court of justice. The difference is that the Christian pictures the case to be tried as a criminal case with himself in the dock; the Jew pictures it as a civil case with himself as the plaintiff. The one hopes for acquittal, or rather for pardon; the other hopes for a resounding triumph with heavy damages."[8]

Too often, we see ourselves as the accused and forget that we have an Advocate who intercedes on our behalf and that the Judge is our heavenly Father (Daniel 7:9, 10, 13, 14; Romans 8:34). This is the good news of the investigative and final judgment: our righteousness is based on Christ's righteousness and our assurance of salvation on His merits, not our own. According to a worldwide survey of Seventh-day Adventists, 70 percent indicated that they have no assurance of salvation.[9] Maybe our image of God as *Judge* needs some revision as we long for this blessed assurance.[10]

As a matter of fact, all three images of God—*Creator, King,* and *Judge*—contribute to this assurance of salvation. He has created us with a plan, a plan of salvation, and He continues to use His creative powers to work His mighty deeds in our life. He is our provider and protector, worthy of praise and service. He is our Redeemer, paying the price that was legally ours through the blood of His Son on the cross. He will vindicate us against all accusations.

Edut—You shall not make yourself an image

We often reduce the second commandment (Exodus 20:4–6) to the fabrication of idols. However, it goes far beyond the physical, including the mental images of who God is and how He is supposed to act. We may see Him as the angry father, the exacting king, or the unforgiving judge. We may see Him as the all-forgiving, hard-of-hearing grandfather who endorses our most misguided wrongdoings, even going as far as to sanctify our basest atrocities (think the Crusades, pogroms, and holocausts of history that were conducted in the name of God). Thus, we ultimately create Him in our own image.

What is your image of God? Karl Barth (1886–1968), a Swiss Reformed theologian who greatly influenced Protestant theology during the twentieth century, called for a return to the Bible. The Reformation's high regard for God's Word was in stark contrast to the prevailing critical view of Scripture. His theology was later described as neo-orthodoxy.

Though I do not necessarily agree with everything Barth taught, his life story is an inspiring testimony to the transforming power of God's Word. He returned to a higher view of Scripture during a time when the Bible had been reduced to a collection of ancient human documents. God had been made in the image of humankind without any power to supernaturally intervene in history (such as the parting of the Red Sea during the Exodus, for example).

Soon after completing his doctoral studies, Barth served as a pastor of a small village church in northern Switzerland, mainly attended by working-class families. There he realized that the God of higher-critical Protestantism had been reduced to a passive deity who had nothing meaningful to say to his parishioners in their toils of daily life. During that time, Barth wrote a commentary on the Epistle to the Romans[11] in which he coined one of his distinctive phrases describing "God as the wholly other," which points to God's complete otherness. While higher criticism had made God subject to humankind, Barth wanted to lead people back to a sovereign God, a God who does not conform to our expectations and well-formulated ideas about Him.

The psalmists of three thousand years ago understood this truth, and they let God speak for Himself through His revelation of images, as divergent as the list of metaphors above. However, they portray a God who is Lord over our past, present, and future, worthy to be served and to be trusted, faithful in His never-ending mercies.

Tehillim—Made in His image

Created in His image
I look at my three sons
They look like me
Though fortunately
Not just like me
But also like their mom.
And then they look
Each one of them
Just like themselves
Coming into their own.
I need to let them
Find their way
And cannot make myself
An image of my sons.
But I can pray
That with each day
God's image they become.

—Martin G. Klingbeil

Psalms

1. Hezekiah's religious reforms recently found an echo in the archaeological record when in 2016 a desecrated gate-shrine was discovered at Tel Lachish in Southern Israel, dated to the time of King Hezekiah. Saar Ganor and Igor Kreimerman, "An Eighth-Century B.C.E. Gate Shrine at Tel Lachish, Israel," *Bulletin of the American Schools of Oriental Research* 381, no. 3 (May 2019): 211–236.

2. See Karel van der Toorn, Bob Becking, and Pieter W. van der Horst, eds., *Dictionary of Deities and Demons in the Bible*, 2nd ed. (Leiden: Brill, 1999).

3. Martin G. Klingbeil, "Psalms 1–75," in *Seventh-day Adventist International Bible Commentary*, ed. Jacques Doukhan, vol. 6, *Psalms, Proverbs, Ecclesiastes, Song of Songs* (Nampa, ID: Pacific Press®/Review and Herald®, 2022), 140.

4. George B. Caird, *The Language and Imagery of the Bible* (Philadelphia, PA: Westminster, 1980), 18.

5. Richard M. Davidson, "The Creation Theme in Psalm 104," in *The Genesis Creation Account and Its Reverberations in the Old Testament*, ed. Gerald A. Klingbeil (Berrien Springs, MI: Andrews University Press, 2015), 150.

6. B. J. Parker, "The Restoration of Shalom: An Intertextual Reading of Leviticus 16 and Psalm 65," *Evangelical Quarterly* 87, no. 3 (2015): 252–263; see also Klingbeil, "Psalms 1–75," 265–269.

7. Paul Copan and Matthew Flannagan, *Did God Really Command Genocide? Coming to Terms With the Justice of God* (Grand Rapids, MI: Baker Books, 2014).

8. C. S. Lewis, *Reflections on the Psalms* (New York: HarperCollins, 2017), 10.

9. "Three Strategic Issues: A World Survey" (Institute of World Mission, Andrews University, 2002).

10. For a short biblical guide to the assurance of salvation, see Ekkehardt Mueller, "Certainty in an Uncertain World?," https://www.adventistbiblicalresearch.org/wp-content/uploads/Certainty-in-an-Uncertain-World_0.pdf.

11. Karl Barth, *Epistle to the Romans*, trans. E. C. Hoskyns (London: Oxford University Press, 1976).

4

The Lord Hears and Delivers

The City of David has a fascinating history and is still a religious center for Jews, Christians, and Muslims. One memory that ancient and modern travelers take with them after visiting Jerusalem is the constant up-and-down walking that it takes to get through the city. If you want to visit the Temple Mount, you need to walk up flights of stairs or narrow ascents. If you want to visit the Mount of Olives, you have to descend into the Kidron Valley and then start the steep climb up to Gethsemane—and then continue farther up to reach the top of the Mount of Olives. From anywhere in Israel, you will eventually have to go up to get to Jerusalem.

In biblical times, during the three annual feasts—the Feast of Unleavened Bread, the Feast of Weeks, and the Feast of Tabernacles (Deuteronomy 16:16), pilgrims from all over Israel and beyond made the long trip up to Jerusalem to worship at the temple. Their upward journey eventually led them past the Pool of Siloam and ended at the southern steps leading up to the city wall.

On the western and eastern sides of the enormous step structure (about 200 feet/61 meters in length) were two gates, one on the western side and one on the eastern side of the stairs. They provided an entrance to the Temple Mount as well as an exit, facilitating the flow of pilgrims through the temple precincts. Today, both gates, named after the prophetess Huldah (2 Kings 22:14; 2 Chronicles 34:22), are blocked,[1] and the interior gateways that used to lead up to the top of the Temple Mount have been redirected and repurposed for the Muslim religious sites located on the mount.

The stairs, initially excavated by Benjamin Mazar in 1967, now form part of the Jerusalem Archaeological Park, close to the City of David excavation project.[2] They consist of fifteen fairly wide steps (35 inches/90 cm) that are interrupted by two narrow steps (12 inches/30 cm), providing fifteen wider spaces where ancient rabbis could have pronounced their doctrines or even where Jesus could have taught the people (Luke 21:37, 38). There are fifteen pilgrim songs in the book of Psalms, also known as the Songs of Ascents (Psalms 120–134), and the suggestion, among others, has been made that those fifteen songs were sung one by one on each successive wider step.[3]

This tradition is still very much alive, and as visitors walk up the southern steps and pause on each wider step, reciting the Songs of Ascents, one can still hear the beautiful words of the psalmists as they wrote about deliverance from bondage and the secret of living together in harmony as a community of faith.

Davar—Songs of Ascents

The historical context of the Songs of Ascents (Psalms 120–134), also known as the Pilgrim Psalms, is the time when Israel returned from the Babylonian exile around 535 BC. All fifteen poems bear the title *shir hamma‘a lot*, meaning "Song of Ascents," pointing to their use as pilgrim songs when ancient Israelites traveled to Jerusalem after returning from Babylon or, later on, during the yearly feasts. These songs reflect a time of renewal and reorientation, and they were written with the purpose of describing Israel's spiritual ascent after the century-long degradation that led to the years of captivity in Babylon.

Among this group are a number of earlier Davidic psalms (Psalms 122; 124; 131; 133), which were most likely applied to the postexilic situation and, based on their contents, included with the pilgrim songs by the final editor of the Psalter, possibly Ezra, the scribe. These songs also lent themselves to be memorized and sung during the yearly journeys up to Jerusalem as they are short, with an average length of seven verses, ranging from three (Psalms 131; 133; 134) to eighteen verses (Psalm 132).

While there are a number of stylistic and literary features that distinguish the Songs of Ascents from the remainder of the psalms (e.g., the scarcity of parallelism and the frequent usage of anadiplosis[4]), the two most striking common traits in these poems are the repeated vocabulary and recurring scenes that echo the theological meaning of the pilgrim psalms. These qualities point to their significance for the postexilic community, which tried to live together in harmony with each other and with God, finding their way back from the Babylonian diaspora to their own land and their own faith (Psalms 120; 121).

Interestingly, Ezra 7:9 describes the journey from Babylon to Jerusalem as an "ascent" (*ma'alah* in Hebrew)—the same term that is used in the title of Psalms 120–134. The five most frequently used key words in the Songs of Ascents are *Israel* (nine times in Psalms 121:4; 122:4; 124:1; 125:5; 128:6; 129:1; 130:7, 8; 131:3), *Zion* (seven times in Psalms 125:1; 126:1; 128:5; 129:5; 132:13; 133:3; 134:3), *Jerusalem* (five times in Psalms 122:2, 3, 6; 125:2; 128:5), *bless/blessed/blessing* (nine times in Psalms 124:6; 128:4, 5; 129:8 [twice]; 132:15; 134:1–3), and *peace* (seven times in Psalms 120:6, 7; 122:6–8; 125:5; 128:6).

The recurring scenes are primarily connected to the daily life in ancient Israel: "slaves watching their master's gesture (Ps 123); people sowing and reaping (Ps 126); men discussing at the city gate (Ps 127); children sitting around the table (Ps 128); an infant at rest with its mother (Ps 131)."[5] This is where the message of the Songs of Ascents is situated: between a city gate somewhere in *Israel* and the temple gates in *Jerusalem*; between the farmer's field and *Zion*; between a nursing child and *peace*; and, ultimately, between a family meal and divine *blessings*. The following provides a few snapshots of these messages.

Psalm 122 possibly captures best the connection between community and cult, between daily life somewhere in an Israelite village and the religious celebrations in the temple precincts on Mount Zion. The psalm is permeated by two words that sound similar in Hebrew, *Jerusalem* (*yerushalaim*) and *peace* (*shalom*). They are symmetrically distributed throughout the psalm, with *Jerusalem* occurring twice (Psalm 122:2, 3) in the first part of the poem, describing the ascent of the tribes to Jerusalem and the temple (verses 1–4), while, correspondingly, *peace* is again mentioned twice (verses 7, 8) in the second part, describing a pilgrim transformed through the temple visit (verses 6–9). *Jerusalem* and *peace* are mentioned together in verse 6 as an invitation to "pray for the peace of Jerusalem." This transformation is possible through what takes place at the center of the psalm (verse 5), a judgment scene reminiscent of Daniel 7:9, 10. The whole psalm is framed by references to the temple (*beit yhwh* "house of the Lord"—Psalm 122:1, 9). Judgment, from the psalmist's perspective, brings transformation and, ultimately, *shalom*, "an all-encompassing concept of well-being that includes physical, emotional, and spiritual aspects."[6] Jesus quotes from Psalm 122 in Luke 19:42 during his triumphal entry to Jerusalem (the ascent—Luke 19:35–42), followed by His announcement of the destruction of Jerusalem and the cleansing of the temple (the judgment scene—verses 43–46), after which Jesus restores *shalom* to the temple through teaching (verse 47), healing (Matthew 21:14), and praise (verse 15), corresponding to the transformation scene of Psalm 122.

The remaining pilgrim psalms provide more detail on both the ascent to Jerusalem (Psalms 123–125) and the transformation resulting from the temple visit after the pilgrims return to their communities and resume their daily lives (Psalms 126–134).

Psalm 123 provides an even higher ascent in that it moves the perspective from the mountain, Mount Zion, to the master, to God Himself. It is Yahweh who is the only One who can rescue and provide true help (Psalm 124). This help, based on a new rule, includes freedom after seventy years of captivity and a charter that recalls the land allotment during the conquest (Psalm 125). Psalm 126 transitions to the effects of the return from captivity, which is almost like a dream as the country transforms and tears turn into joy. Houses and families are built in Psalm 127, and Psalm 128 elaborates on the fruit of hard labor, a blessing that ultimately comes from Zion. There is no more exploitation and bondage as Yahweh cuts the cords of the wicked (Psalm 129).

Psalms 130–134 portray the restoration of the inner person: there is a need for divine forgiveness (Psalm 130) and a renewed hope in the Lord (Psalm 131) based on the remembrance of David, whose reign serves as an ideal paradigm for a restored Israel (Psalm 132). Psalm 133 points to the blessings of a community that lives together in harmony, and the final Song of Ascents, Psalm 134, is a farewell blessing, a blessing that could have been sung at the culmination of the temple services before the pilgrims started the journey back to their homes.

Pesher—How beautiful when brothers dwell together

When our three boys were younger and would occasionally squabble, I would sometimes start singing a Hebrew song that I had taught them: *hinneh mah tov umah na'im shevet akhim gam yakhad* "Behold, how good and pleasant it is when brothers dwell in unity!" (Psalm 133:1, ESV). Occasionally, it would work, and the three of them would eventually join me in singing, forgetting their quarrel for a moment. Psalm 133 perfectly embodies the theological message of the Songs of Ascents.

Brotherly unity is both "good and pleasant," and the combination of these two terms describe God and His name elsewhere in the Psalms (Psalm 135:3), indicating that unity begins with God. While the idea of dwelling together certainly applies to the postexilic community that needed to learn once more to live together in harmony (it appears that more than just the southern tribes returned from exile—Ezra 2:70; 6:17), the Hebrew word *yashab*, translated "dwell" in Psalm 133:1, should rather be translated here as "sit," describing a festive gathering along the lines of the banquet in Psalm 23:5, 6. This fits the context of the Songs of Ascents, as Israelites traveled, camped, and ate together on their way up to Jerusalem.

Two comparisons anchor Israel's unity in the temple worship in Jerusalem and the accompanying blessings of Yahweh. The aromatic oil (Psalm 133:2) alludes to the anointing of Aaron (Exodus 29; Leviticus 8) and the inauguration of the temple services. As the oil runs down Aaron's head and beard, "it drips down and naturally flows onto the clothing of the priest, which includes the ephod and breastplate containing the names of the twelve tribes,"[7] thus extending the blessings received during the yearly feasts from the pilgrims to the whole community.

The second comparison (Psalm 133:3) links Mount Hermon in the far north of Israel with Mount Zion in Jerusalem. This is theological topography, and the heavenly dew that provides moisture to dry land, and thus fertility (Deuteronomy 33:13), reunites the north (Israel) and the south (Judah), while Zion receives preference because "there the LORD commanded the blessing" (Psalm 133:3).

Scholars have long recognized the frequent allusions to the Aaronic blessing (Numbers 6:24–26) in the Songs of Ascents.[8] Interestingly, the fifteen Hebrew words in the Aaronic blessing correspond to the number of Pilgrim Psalms and the southern steps. Beyond this numerical connection, Aaron's blessing served as the theological paradigm for a postexilic community that needed to relearn how to live together in harmony under Yahweh's *shalom*. Unity is possible only by meeting in God's presence.

Edut—The church after COVID

Coming back from COVID has sometimes felt a bit like returning from exile. Our Zoom-connected living often reduced church to a weekly two-hour media event. And then came the polarizing vaccine discussions that fragmented church congregations. How does one rebuild or even build a new thriving community of faith? The Songs of Ascents provide valuable biblical pointers that can be meaningful in modern times.

The Pilgrim Psalms arise from the interplay between daily life and cult, between villages somewhere in Israel and the temple in Jerusalem. Church takes place on the mountain (Mount Zion: Psalms 121–126) as well as in a field where a community plows together and eats the fruit of their labor (Psalm 126, 127), or among olive groves that a family harvests (Psalm 128). It takes place when we stand up against exploitation (Psalm 129) and when we receive forgiveness (Psalm 130). It can even happen when a mother soothes her child with a lullaby (Psalm 131) or when we learn to live together in harmony (Psalm 133).

Maybe the problem is rather that we have disassociated our daily lives from the realm of the church. As the Israelites traveled together for days, maybe even weeks, to go up to Jerusalem, they did so in groups for reasons of safety and, foremost, community. Along the way, they learned to get along with each other, look out for each other, and even sing together the Songs of Ascents in harmony. Interestingly, Mary and Joseph only looked for Jesus on the second day after they had left the feast in Jerusalem, trusting their fellow pilgrims to such an extent that they assumed that their boy was somewhere safe among their group of travelers (Luke 2:43–45). Our communities of faith need to live together as much in our daily journeys as we do on Sabbath in church.[9]

The Songs of Ascents powerfully point us back to God's blessings. The rehearsing of and allusions to the Aaronic blessing (Numbers 6:24–26) in Psalms 120–134 highlight the continuous divine blessings that begin through an encounter with God in the temple and flow out from there like the oil that flows down Aaron's beard, onto the pilgrims, and through them into every corner of the land—a beautiful image for the church today.

Tehillim—Connectedness

> How wonderful, how beautiful,
> > when brothers and sisters get along!
> It's like costly anointing oil
> > flowing down head and beard,
> Flowing down Aaron's beard,
> > flowing down the collar of his priestly robes.
> It's like the dew on Mount Hermon
> > flowing down the slopes of Zion.
> Yes, that's where God commands the blessing,
> > ordains eternal life (Psalm 133, *The Message*).

---

1. The western Huldah gate is only partially blocked, and its western portal serves as an entry to the Fatimid tower, where the al-Khatuniyya library is housed.

2. For more information on these excavations, visit the Jerusalem Archaeological Park website at http://www.archpark.org.il.

3. The *Mishnah*, the first written postbiblical record of Jewish oral law codified around AD 200, suggests that the Songs of Ascents were sung by the Levites during the Feast of Booths (*Sukkot*) standing on the fifteen steps that lead from the women's court up to the Israelites' court in the temple precincts (*m. Sukkah* 5:4, 5).

4. Parallelism (or *parallelismus membrorum*) is a form of repetition between successive poetic lines (see chapter 1) and, as such, is the most distinguishing feature of Hebrew poetry. Anadiplosis is step technique, where the last word of a line is repeated as the first word in the next line. Martin G. Klingbeil, "Introduction to Hebrew Poetry and Wisdom Books," in *Andrews Bible Commentary: Light. Depth. Truth.*, ed. Ángel Manuel Rodríguez (Berrien Springs, MI: Andrews University Press, 2020), 1:614–623.

5. Th. Booij, "Psalms 120–136: Songs for a Great Festival," *Biblica* 91, no. 2 (2010): 243.

6. Martin G. Klingbeil, "Psalms," in Rodriguez, *Andrews Bible Commentary*, 744.

7. Klingbeil, 749.

8. Leon J. Liebreich, "The Songs of Ascents and the Priestly Blessing," *Journal of Biblical Literature* 74, no. 1 (1955): 33–36.

9. Peter Roennfeldt, *Your Church Has Changed: Rebuilding Church and Mission Post-COVID-19* (Warburton, Australia: Signs Publishing, 2021).

5

Singing the Lord's Song in a Strange Land

Feelings of being lonely, lost, abandoned, and afraid are among the most traumatic emotions we humans can experience. While working at Helderberg College, the Seventh-day Adventist tertiary education institution at the southern tip of Africa, I took my family on a shopping trip to the local mall on a busy Sunday morning in South Africa. Our son David, a curious yet very shy two-year-old, was with us. At the end of our grocery shopping, we were pushing a full shopping cart ("trolley" in South African) into a small shoe shop to look at some shoes for my wife, Thandi. I held the hand of our oldest son, Jonathan, and my wife held David's hand. At some point, she let go of his hand to try on a pair of shoes, and by the time we looked up, our quick little David was gone from the shop, out into the flow of humanity that was streaming through the mall. Quickly, we decided that I would run left toward the entrance and parking lots while my wife would go right back into the mall with our other son, leaving the shopping cart with a very sympathetic salesperson. As I was running left, desperately scanning the crowds for our blond-haired little boy, my worst fears began to materialize in my mind: a car accident outside, a child kidnapping, a small child wandering out into a hostile environment.

I couldn't find him and decided that he could not have gone far in the few minutes since we had lost him, so I frantically turned back into the mall to look for Thandi and my boys. I eventually found all of them on a little bench along the wall where the mall turned a corner, in one big embrace with everybody's tears rolling freely. Jonathan had one shoe in his hand that he had lost as Mommy had dragged him along in her frantic sprint down the mall corridor. I joined in the hugs and tears as we pieced together what had happened.

David had walked out of the shop, turned right, and walked until he realized that he was alone and lost among people he did not know. Then Mommy saw him just as he was turning the corner and screamed his name, breaking into a desperate sprint while dragging Jonathan behind. As she snatched him up into her arms, he looked into her face and said just one word: "Afraid."

Since Adam and Eve left the Garden (Genesis 3:24), humanity has felt a sense of lostness and loneliness, especially in times of distress. In moments of suffering, sickness, and sorrow, the psalmists have expressed this sense of abandonment, longing for the presence of their heavenly Father and asking the penetrating question: "Why do you hide your face from me?" (Psalm 88:14, ESV) These questions ultimately climax in Jesus' question on the cross, echoing through the universe: "My God, My God, why have You forsaken Me?" (Matthew 27:46).

Davar—Theodicy

God's silence and absence in the face of human suffering is a topic that concerned the psalmists of three thousand years ago. Their psalms are replete with expressions that point to the authors' struggle with God's perceived absence.

God hiding His face (Psalms 10:11; 13:1; 22:24; 27:9; 30:7; 44:24; 69:17; 88:14; 89:46; 102:2; 104:29; 143:7) points to the feeling of utter abandonment and is often connected to His forgetting (Psalms 31:12; 42:9;

44:24; 74:19; 77:9; 78:11), which is not divine memory loss but the human experience of losing God's favor and being barred from His presence.

God being silent (Psalms 28:1; 35:22; 39:12; 50:3; 83:1; 109:1) and not hearing the psalmist's cries (Psalms 22:2; 66:18) are further attempts to come to terms with suffering in the face of apparent divine distance. However, almost all of these expressions are phrased as questions. The "How long?" question is the most prevalent one (Psalms 6:3; 13:2; 35:17; 74:10; 79:5; 80:4; 82:2; 89:46; 90:13; 94:3) and indicates how the psalmists ultimately believed their suffering to be a temporary wilderness experience (Psalms 55:7; 63:1; 102:6; 107:4; 136:16), an experience delimited by divine grace and guaranteed reversal when God hears again and turns His face toward the petitioner, and the psalmist once more experiences closeness with God (Psalm 63:8). Feeling God's absence was very real to the psalmists, even described in the suffering of the Messiah in Psalm 22. The poem begins with the universe-piercing question of God's abandonment of Jesus on the cross. "My God, My God, why have you forsaken me?" (verse 1).

Theodicy (Latin, meaning "justifying God") asks the question of how a good God can tolerate innocent suffering. It ultimately aims at vindicating divine goodness and providing a defense for a just and loving God. Not that a sovereign God needs any human defending, but the question of why the just suffer and the wicked prosper is as old as the world after the Fall. It is central to the book of Job, considered one of the earliest books of the Old Testament.[1] Job's life provides an extended engagement with the question of theodicy, coming to an interesting conclusion in Job 42:5: "My ears had heard of you but now my eyes have seen you" (NIV). In the final analysis, theodicy is an existential crisis of our own personal faith and how we see the character of God.[2]

Two psalms are of particular interest for the question of theodicy: Psalms 88 and 73. Both reflect the psalmist's struggle with their suffering while God seems to be gone.

Singing the Lord's Song in a Strange Land

Psalm 88 presents a gloomy picture of utter darkness and stands out in the long list of psalms that deal with divine silence. There seems to be no hope, not even at the end of the psalm, where we often find a glimpse of hope as in other theodicy psalms (e.g., Psalm 22:22–31).

The first section of Psalm 88 deals with the affliction and suffering the psalmist is facing, painting a picture of imminent death with mention of the grave, the pit, darkness, and God's wrath rolling over him without any hope of escape (verses 1–9). This leads to a series of rhetorical questions about death that appeal to God's mercy, faithfulness, and righteousness (verses 10–12). The last part of the psalm (verses 13–18) begins with the hopeful expression "in the morning" (verse 13), a positive turnaround in other psalms (e.g., Psalms 5:3; 30:5; 46:5), but in this case, it is the opposite—the psalmist is confronted with more suffering that seems to overwhelm him like a flood. The last word of Psalm 88 in the original language is "darkness," ending the poem on a note of despair. Sometimes there is no resolution to suffering, then or now. There are no easy answers to the question of theodicy because God will not always reverse our suffering on this side of eternity.[3]

As part of the group of Asaph psalms (Psalms 73–83) at the beginning of Book III, Psalm 73 raises the question of theodicy in an explicit way. This group of psalms is centered on the question "God, where are you?" and deals with it from a communal and individual perspective.

It is difficult for Asaph to reconcile the prosperity of the wicked and the suffering of the just (Psalm 73:2–5). However, he finds answers in a surprising place. Going beyond apologetics (i.e., defending God), he identifies life-applicable wisdom in the greater picture. For the psalmist, the prosperity of the wicked becomes an obstacle in his spiritual journey (verse 13), something that he cannot understand (verse 16). Why should he remain pure? His query is the somewhat futile question of the righteous man who has cleansed his heart in vain and is trying to live a life of integrity in the face of adversity.

The turning point came when he "went into the sanctuary of God" (verse 17). Only through entering the sanctuary does he begin to understand where it all ends; he begins to see the bigger picture. Our perspective is often limited and tends to focus on this side of eternity. By entering into God's presence, the psalmist grasps the fleeting appeal of the evildoers' prosperity as their feet are set in "slippery places" (verse 18) and notes that they are "destroyed in a moment" (verse 19, ESV). Sometimes it is essential to look at the future to make sense of the present, especially if this future is centered on God. For the psalmist, the future is glorious because it moves toward an eternal and existential relationship with his God: "Whom have I in heaven but You?" (verse 25). Maybe this is the ultimate answer to the question of theodicy, bringing us back to Job's declaration, "I have heard of You by the hearing of the ear, but now my eye sees You" (Job 42:5). This intimate relationship with God is what helps us realize that He is all we need, no matter the circumstances.

Asaph understood this by entering the sanctuary, and as he wrote about his experience, he designed his poem to reflect his newfound insights into the character of God. The Hebrew word *tob* ("good") frames the psalm (Psalm 73:1, 28). This framing is a literary device called an *inclusio*, pointing to the principal premise that God is good. At the end of the psalm, "it is good to be near God" indicates that God's goodness translates into our own good as we draw nearer to Him. And finally, "there is also a reversal of fates: whereas the psalmist finds himself on slippery ground (73:1–3) and the wicked are secure (73:4–12), it is the wicked who are later slipping (73:18–20), and the psalmist is on firm ground in God's presence (73:28) at the end of the poem."[4]

Pesher—Darkness and Light

I recently had the privilege of serving as the external examiner of a PhD dissertation defense at McMasters Divinity College in Canada. With an intriguing title ("Where Is the Place of Darkness: A Metaphor Analysis of Darkness in the Old Testament")[5] and a thorough study of the metaphor of darkness, the author comes to the conclusion that the idea "EVIL IS DARKNESS is foreign to the OT" and that while darkness in the Old Testament is associated with death and captivity, it is also connected to Yahweh: He wields it (Exodus 10:21–29; 14:20; Deuteronomy 28:28, 29; Psalm 105:28), stands upon it (Psalm 18:9–11; cf. 2 Samuel 22:10–12), and even dwells in it (Exodus 19; 20; 1 Kings 8:10–12; Psalm 97:2), thus demonstrating His sovereignty over it. In fact, the dissertation makes a strong case that the idea of a dualism between light (= good) and dark (= evil) is foreign to the biblical worldview and has its origin in Persian Zoroastrianism and Greek mythology/philosophy that made inroads into Judaism during the intertestamental period and into Christianity during the second and third centuries AD, respectively. The biblical worldview is rather theocentric than dualistic and puts a sovereign God at the center of everything.

This implies a completely different understanding of the question of theodicy and human suffering. It is in the valley of the shadow of death that David finds his personal Divine Shepherd.[6] It is through the darkness of human suffering that Job forms a more intimate relationship with his Redeemer, who is completely in control of what Satan can and cannot do to Job. Satan's evil intentions are foiled because God uses darkness to come close to His suffering children.

Edut—"Eli, Eli, lama sabachthani?"

Christ's forlorn cry from Calvary makes it appear that Satan has triumphed at last. Christ hangs between heaven and earth in the center of three crosses. The few disciples who have dared to follow their teacher up to this moment watch their hopes dissolve amidst the sufferings of the Son of God. The victory of evil seems imminent. Nature has hidden itself under a cloak of darkness and suffers together with its Creator. Even God seems to be silent and absent: "And about three o'clock Jesus cried with a loud voice, 'Eli, Eli, lama sabachthani?' that is, 'My God, my God, why have you forsaken me?' " (Matthew 27:46, NRSV).

Jesus' desperate words seem to point to His Father's absence. Yet there is another perspective to this depressing scene: "With amazement angels witnessed the Saviour's despairing agony. The hosts of heaven veiled their faces from the fearful sight. Inanimate nature expressed sympathy with its insulted and dying Author. The sun refused to look upon the awful scene. Its full, bright rays were illuminating the earth at midday, when suddenly it seemed to be blotted out. Complete darkness, like a funeral pall, enveloped the cross."[7] This darkness seems to point to God's absence in this pivotal moment of salvation history. But Ellen G. White continues, "In that thick darkness God's presence was hidden. He makes darkness His pavilion, and conceals His glory from human eyes. God and His holy angels were beside the cross. The Father was with His Son."[8]

That which at first sight appeared to be the victory of evil was, in reality, the turning point in the plan of salvation, making it possible for humankind to return to God. The Father suffered with His Son. The apparent defeat is the actual victory. One only needs a change of perspective. God's perceived absence is never a real absence.

The famous illustration of the footprints in the sand still holds true. A man who dreams about the scenes of his life sees two sets of footprints in the sand, one of them his and the other God's. However, during the difficult moments of his life, there is suddenly only one set of footprints. He turns to his heavenly Father, asking Him why he was left alone during these times of trial and suffering, to which God replies, "These were the times when I carried you in My arms." Today, He still carries us. He is just where He always has been, close to His suffering children.

Tehillim—From darkness to dawn

Reach us, Jesus, from Your cross,
Though we feel forsaken;
Keep us through the aching night
Till new dawns awaken.[9]

1. "The long years spent amid desert solitudes were not lost. Not only was Moses gaining a preparation for the great work before him, but during this time, under the inspiration of the Holy Spirit, he wrote the book of Genesis and also the book of Job, which would be read with the deepest interest by the people of God until the close of time." Ellen G. White, "Moses," *Signs of the Times*, February 19, 1880, [1].

2. Fredrik Lindström, "Theodicy in the Psalms," in *Theodicy in the World of the Bible*, ed. Antti Laato and Johannes C. de Moor (Boston: Brill, 2003), 256–303.

3. Martin G. Klingbeil, "Psalms," in *Andrews Bible Commentary. Light. Depth. Truth.*, ed. Ángel Manuel Rodríguez (Berrien Springs, MI: Andrews University Press, 2020), 1:718, 719.

4. Martin G. Klingbeil, "Psalms 1-75," in *Seventh-day Adventist International Bible Commentary*, ed. Jacques Doukhan, vol. 6, *Psalms, Proverbs, Ecclesiastes, Song of Songs* (Nampa, ID: Pacific Press®, 2022), 300.

5. Daniel Ross Cooper, "Where Is the Place of Darkness: A Metaphor Analysis of Darkness in the Old Testament" (PhD dissertation; McMaster Divinity College, Hamilton, ON, Canada, 2021).

6. See chapter 2.

7. Ellen G. White, *The Desire of Ages* (Mountain View, CA: Pacific Press®, 1940), 753.

8. White, 753, 754.

9. Brian Wren, "When on Life a Darkness Falls" (Carol Stream, IL: Hope Publishing, 1985).

6

I Will Arise

The following story is *not* true, but unfortunately, similar stories abound without and within the church. It has been composed against the background of a number of true stories that I have sadly witnessed during my pastoral and teaching ministry. They occur again and again, painfully present and pervasive in every culture and geographical region on this globe.

Christine had been suffering in silence for far too long. Her silence had impacted her health as she was fighting depression and eating disorders. It had delayed any form of healing from the abuse she had experienced during her teenage years and had negatively impacted her desperate attempt to build normal and healthy relationships. The desperate truth was that her silence was far from being her own choice; she had been vociferously silenced whenever she had tried to speak out. It had been the pastor of her church who, during her Pathfinder years, had sexually abused her. He had sworn her to secrecy, threatening suicide if she would mention anything to anybody. She had felt guilty, dirty, and hopeless.

After the pastor eventually confessed to the church board in order to redeem his ministry, she thought that now there might be an opportunity to speak out and find healing. Instead, her parents were disappointed in her, doubting the veracity of her words. She was dragged in front of the church board to acknowledge her own part in the committed sin. It was one continuous nightmare from which there was no awakening.

Eventually, she moved far away, and the pastor was transferred to another church. Years later, while studying at an Adventist university, she learned that the perpetrator, by that time, not a minister anymore, had moved into the local community. She had wanted to leave all of the darkness behind. She had just gotten engaged to a young ministerial student who walked with her along the road of healing. Now, suddenly, the whole nightmare came rolling back. However, this time, she found herself in a community that listened when she spoke out, and action was taken to prevent the perpetrator from repeating his destructive behavior.

More important, she found a Christian counselor who helped her process her deep hurt and find healing through, among other counseling techniques, reading a group of psalms. Those initially did not seem to have anything to do with her traumatic experiences. In fact, at first, she felt repelled by the strong statements made in these psalms, which included curses, imprecations, and bloodthirsty wishes for vengeance and retribution. But, strangely enough, they provided timely help, and healing was able to begin.

Davar—Smashing babies against rocks?

This sad story illustrates the strong emotions that people experience when faced with tragedy and disappointment. The poetry of Psalm 137 speaks powerfully to these feelings. It highlights resistance against ridicule and blasphemy, the strength of collective memory, and hope in the face of tragedy—until one reads the last two verses: "O daughter of Babylon, doomed to be destroyed, blessed shall he be who repays you with what you have done to us! Blessed shall he be who takes your little ones and dashes them against the rock!" (verses 8, 9, ESV).

Psalms

This is one of the most disturbing beatitudes[1] in Scripture. It challenges our understanding of inspiration and our notions of a God of love. Bible interpreters have struggled to understand these and similar verses throughout the book of Psalms.

Before looking at the bigger picture of these texts, it might be important to consider the context of these two verses. Psalm 137 has a number of historical and geographical references (verses 1, 5–8) evoking the traumatic experiences of the Babylonian exile (605–535 BC), and it was written either during this period or, more likely, from a postexilic perspective in hindsight. It starts with the haunting memories of the Babylonian captivity and the blasphemous taunting of the oppressors (verses 1–3), followed by a call to resistance based on the memories of Jerusalem (verses 4–6). The psalm concludes with a petition for God to remember (the Hebrew verb *zakar*, meaning "to remember," occurs once in each of the three sections—verses 1, 6, 7) all of these atrocities and provide justice (verses 7–9).

In verse 7, there is a further geographical marker beyond Babylon and Jerusalem, referring to Edom's part in the events that surrounded the fall of Jerusalem at the beginning of the Babylonian exile. In 586 BC, Edomite mercenaries, who had made an alliance with Nebuchadnezzar to hand over the fleeing Judeans to their Babylonian captors, rounded up Judean refugees who had escaped the besieged city of Jerusalem and were trying to cross the river Jordan to safety (Obadiah 8–15). The Edomites, of course, were descendants of Esau and thus brothers to the people of Israel (verses 10–12).[2]

This historical backdrop to the psalm helps us understand the poem's strong emotions and its concluding call for vengeance. It recalls unspeakable atrocities that took place at the beginning and throughout the Babylonian exile as the Israelites were struggling to process the trauma of war and captivity after their return to Jerusalem. They were trying to find a way forward by bringing those events before God and appealing to

Him to "remember" what they themselves were not able to forget. God's remembrance in the Old Testament is more than a cognitive process that brings something back to mind; it is rather related to an action that is often followed by deliverance.

When God remembers Noah in the ark, the waters begin to recede (Genesis 8:1); when He remembers Rachel, she conceives and Joseph is born (Genesis 30:22–24), and when He remembers his covenant, Moses is called and the Exodus begins (Exodus 6:5–8). In the Psalms, God is often called upon to remember (Psalms 9:12; 25:6, 7; 74:2, 18, 22; 79:8; 89:47; 98:3; 132:1; 137:7), and it is always a call for Him to act on behalf of His people. Thus, the call for God in Psalm 137:7 to remember asks Him to provide justice and to correct the wrongs described in this psalm.[3]

Pesher—Imprecation and inspiration

Psalm 137 does not stand alone with its calls for retribution. Other imprecatory, cursing, or vengeance psalms request God to "slay the wicked" (Psalm 139:19), "cast them out" (Psalm 5:10), "let them be clothed with shame" (Psalm 35:26), "give to them according to their work" (Psalm 28:4, ESV), "let them go down alive into Sheol" (Psalm 55:15, ASV), "break the teeth in their mouths" (Psalm 58:6, ESV), "consume them in wrath" (Psalm 59:13), "let them be blotted out of the book of the living" (Psalm 69:28), "deal with them as . . . with Sisera" (Psalm 83:9),[4] and "let his children continually be vagabonds, and beg" (Psalm 109:10). It would be more correct to talk about imprecatory passages within psalms, including those that cover a variety of other topics, rather than focus on complete imprecatory psalms.

Interpreters have struggled with these passages for centuries because they appear to portray a picture of God that is incompatible with the principle of Christian love for our enemies (Matthew 5:43, 44). The destruction they urge is nothing we would wish on anyone. But what happens if we do?

Luther understood these passages as messianic and saw Jesus, allegorically, as the speaker and the victim, with the Jews being the perpetrators—a difficult position to maintain, taking into consideration, for example, the clear historical context found in Psalm 137.[5] Modern interpreters have questioned the inspiration of these psalms, suggesting that these passages, or any other uncomfortable passages of the Old Testament for that matter, represent a primitive, pre- or sub-Christian view of God. Others have discarded them completely by relegating them to the dispensation of law, which has been done away with under the new dispensation of grace inaugurated by Christ. Still others suggest that this is hyperbolic speech or poetic language that should not be taken literally.[6] What these suggestions have in common is that they question the inspiration of Scripture (2 Timothy 3:16, 17) and challenge the unchangeability of God (Malachi 3:6), ultimately leaving it up to the human individual to decide what is and what is not inspired in Scripture.

From a perspective of *tota scriptura* (the totality of Scripture), one of the three principles of biblical interpretation derived from the Protestant Reformation, there are no degrees of inspiration within the Bible. David claims inspiration for his psalms (2 Samuel 23:1–3), the psalms themselves report God's speech (e.g., Psalm 12:5, 6), and when Jesus quotes from the psalms in the New Testament, confirming their inspiration and place in the canon, the imprecatory passages are included (e.g., John 15:25). Thus, these psalms appear to serve particular theological and practical purposes within the Bible.

One characteristic the vengeance psalms have in common is their usage of *legal terminology*. There is mention of the covenant and curses associated with the breaking of it (compare Psalm 69:23 with Deuteronomy 28:22, 28), invoking God as Judge and asking for divine retribution (Psalm 35:23, 24).

Other legal expressions include "pronounce them guilty" (Psalm 5:10), "the righteous . . . sees the vengeance" (Psalm 58:10), and "let an accuser stand at his right hand" (Psalm 109:6). The Hebrew word *naqam*, usually translated as "vengeance," is part of divine-judgment terminology and is better translated as "just retribution" in the context of vindicating the oppressed. Deuteronomy 32:35 clarifies that retribution belongs to God ("vengeance is Mine"), not to humans, and that it is part of fair judgment (verse 41).

Furthermore, divine retribution is governed by the *lex talionis* (law of retribution), which provides for a punishment that is proportionate to the offense. The cursing psalms ask exactly for this: "Give to them according to their work and according to the evil of their deeds" (Psalm 28:4, ESV). Human vengeance is intrinsically disproportionate and bound to escalate the conflict. Verbal skirmishes can lead to nuclear wars. To protect against this tendency, the Bible gives detailed prohibitions against humans taking revenge (Genesis 4:15; Leviticus 19:18; 1 Samuel 24:12; Ezekiel 25:15; Romans 12:19, 20). Thus, the imprecatory psalms call on God to intervene on behalf of Israel instead of Israel seeking their own revenge and retribution, even if those feelings are justified.

Indignation is not a popular word in modern culture. Instead, tolerance has become the ideal when dealing with difficult issues. Tolerance, however, ends in absolute relativism, where right or wrong does not exist anymore. Indignation is rightful anger against unfair treatment and moral evil.

The historical context of Psalm 137:7–9 provides a vivid background for the indignation that the Jewish exiles felt toward the Babylonian taunts and blasphemies, which were ultimately directed against the God of Israel. Conquering a nation in the ancient Near East also meant conquering their gods (2 Kings 18:33–35; Daniel 3:15). The reference to a "foreign land" in Psalm 137:4 can be a reference to foreign gods because the Hebrew *nekar* "foreign" is often used in cultic contexts that contrast the true God with foreign deities (Deuteronomy 32:12; Jeremiah 5:19). The cursing psalms express Israel's rightful indignation against the atrocities of war, the oppressions experienced in captivity, and the accompanying blasphemies of their God.

And then there is grace. Loving your neighbor and your enemy is not a concept that is foreign to the Old Testament (Leviticus 19:18). In the case of Jonah, he had reason to curse the Ninevites because of the long history of Assyrian atrocities against Israel and other nations. Yet God granted them grace in response to their repentance (Jonah 3:10; Jeremiah 18:5–10). God saw a bigger picture than Jonah did, and He is no less attentive to us. He hears our cries for vengeance, responding to them with justice and mercy as only He can.

Edut—Cursing psalms and Christian counseling

Now back to Christine. The first step in her journey toward healing was the moment when she was able to openly express her feelings of anger, even hate, toward her perpetrator. As she read the cursing psalms, she realized that God allowed these emotions as part of His inspired Word. He heard the desperate cries of the psalmists that matched her own traumatic experiences. Counselors call such cries a "cathartic release of negative emotion,"[7] realizing that the first step to healing is verbalizing the experienced hurt and anger.

The poetic language of the psalms encourages the listener to identify with the words of the psalmists. Their heart-rending expressions are full of vivid imagery: "Let my tongue cling to the roof of my mouth" (Psalm 137:6). They urge immediate action: "Save me, O God! For the waters have come up to my neck" (Psalm 69:1), but they are also paired with expressions of hope: "Then my soul will rejoice in the Lord, exulting in his salvation" (Psalm 35:9, ESV).

Researchers have found that numbing strong emotions of anger can lead to symptoms comparable to combat trauma or post-traumatic stress disorder (PTSD).[8] Frequently, this type of repression can result in psychosomatic disorders or violent behavior toward others as the emotions are looking for a way to be expressed. Previous victimization often leads to victimizing others. When we take vengeance into our own hands, we hurt ourselves or others or both.[9]

The psalms were more than expressions of personal-faith journeys in ancient Israel. They were also intended to be read and recited throughout the millennia, in the synagogue and in the church. The imprecatory passages cannot be excluded from our modern reading of the Psalms, and neither should they be theologically dismissed. The psalmists understood the importance of expressing emotions of hurt, trauma, and anger; yet they also equally understood the importance of handing them over to God. In leaving it up to Him to take care of retribution as the just Judge, they were able to let go of their hurt, move beyond it, heal, and even find forgiveness for the perpetrator, living out the biblical ideal of love for one's enemy (Proverbs 25:21, 22; Luke 6:27, 28).

Tehillim—A Prayer for the Victims

I pray for the
Widow
Orphan
Poor
Homeless
Alien
Wounded
Abused
Refugee
Migrant
Traumatized
Betrayed
Oppressed

Psalms

Lonely

Slave

Stigmatized

May God vindicate

And heal their wounds

—Martin G. Klingbeil

---

1. The Hebrew word *ashre*—"blessed/content/happy are those who"—is used here, which is also the first word of the book of Psalms. Here it is used as part of a most shocking blessing for those who commit atrocities.

2. Martin G. Klingbeil, "Psalms," in *Andrews Bible Commentary. Light. Depth. Truth.*, ed. Angel Manuel Rodríguez (Berrien Springs, MI: Andrews University Press, 2020), 1:751, 752.

3. See Leslie C. Allen, "רכז (# 2349)," in *New International Dictionary of Old Testament Theology & Exegesis*, ed. Moisés Silva (Grand Rapids, MI: Zondervan, 2014), 1:1103, 1104.

4. Sisera, general in the army of Jabin, king of Hazor, was killed by Jael, the wife of Heber the Kenite in the time of the Judges, when Deborah and Barak fought against the Canaanites. She drove a tent peg through Sisera's temple after lulling him to sleep in her tent (Judges 4:17–22; cf. chapter 1).

5. Daniel Michael Nehrbass, *Praying Curses: The Therapeutic and Preaching Value of the Imprecatory Psalms* (Eugene, OR: Pickwick Publications, 2013), 42.

6. For a comprehensive discussion of the theological dimension of the imprecatory psalms, see Angel Manuel Rodriguez, "Inspiration and the Imprecatory Psalms," *Journal of the Adventist Theological Society* 5, no. 1 (1994):40–67. Some of the following observations are drawn from this article.

7. Dominick David Hankle, "The Therapeutic Implications of the Imprecatory Psalms in the Christian Counseling Setting,"abstract, *Journal of Psychology and Theology* 38, no. 4 (2010).

8. Hankle, 277.

9. Walter Brueggemann provides an excellent discussion of the vengeance psalms in the short video "Walter Brueggemann Psalms of Vengeance," YouTube video, posted by Pete Miko, 5:07, February 8, 2010, https://www.youtube.com/watch?v=rDfzzJD8IpI.

7

Your Mercy Reaches Unto the Heavens

The God of the Old Testament has often been contrasted with the God of the New Testament: a God of wrath versus a God who is full of love and mercy. Richard Dawkins, an enthusiastic advocate of atheism, does not mince words in describing the God of the Old Testament: "The God of the Old Testament is arguably the most unpleasant character in all fiction: jealous and proud of it; a petty, unjust, unforgiving control-freak; a vindictive, bloodthirsty ethnic cleanser; a misogynistic, homophobic, racist, infanticidal, genocidal, filicidal, pestilential, megalomaniacal, sadomasochistic, capriciously malevolent bully."[1] While the rhetoric is acrimonious and the author has been criticized even from within the atheist community for his almost religious zeal to discredit a Christian worldview,[2] the question of the character of God in the Old Testament is also prevalent in Christian circles.

Early in the second century AD, Marcion of Sinope, the son of a Christian bishop in Asia Minor, claimed that the malevolent creator God of the Old Testament was opposed to the benevolent God of the New Testament. Consequently, he established his own canon of Scripture, rejecting the entire Old Testament, only accepting a shorter version of the Gospel of Luke and a selection of ten Pauline epistles. He was declared a heretic and excommunicated in AD 144, but his teaching of the discontinuity between the God of the Old and New Testaments has made it into modern Christianity.[3]

It is often urged that the story of the conquest of Canaan illustrates the bloodthirstiness of the Old Testament God. But a careful study of the events shows that God's mercy is powerfully present even in acts of divine judgment and that such acts are always preceded by extended periods of grace—nearly five hundred years in the case of Canaan (Genesis 15:16). Furthermore, God restricted the complete destruction (Hebrew *cherem*, meaning "ban") to a limited number of cities (Joshua 6:24; 8:28; 11:13, 14; Judges 18:27) and punished any abuse of his directive (1 Samuel 15). It served as an act of obedience, a prophylaxis for syncretism, which demonstrated the gravity of sin, and purposed to establish Israel in the Promised Land.[4]

The book of Psalms portrays the same God of the Old Testament. With frequent references to the time of the conquest (e.g., Psalms 16:5, 6; 44:1–8; 60:6–8; etc.), God is portrayed as a God of mercy, a heavenly Father, a Divine Shepherd, a safe Refuge, an eternal Rock, a generous King, and a mighty Fortress whose mercy endures forever (Psalm 136).

Davar—Penitential psalms and David

A number of psalms directly connect with a historical situation narrated elsewhere in Scripture. The title of Psalm 51 reads: "To the Chief Musician. A Psalm of David when Nathan the prophet went to him, after he had gone in to Bathsheba." While the initial note is likely linked with the musical performance of this psalm in the temple worship of ancient Israel, the historical annotation connects the poem with the events of 2 Samuel 11; 12. In the book of Samuel, we read the story in its narrative context (David's adultery with Bathsheba,[5] his plot to kill Uriah, Nathan's parable, David's confession, God's forgiveness) but sometimes miss the inner turmoil, the emotional exhaustion, or the physical consequences of this unconfessed sin in David's life. The book of Psalms includes Psalms 51 and 32 to provide us with insights into the existential crisis that David experienced as a result of his brief but consequential moment of giving in to sexual temptation. These psalms belong to the group of penitential psalms (Psalms 6; 32; 38; 51; 102; 130; 143) that deal with the question of sin and divine forgiveness.

Psalm 51 can be divided into a confession of sin (verses 1–9), followed by an experience of true restoration through forgiveness (verses 10–15), and a return to authentic worship, leaving behind the hollow hypocrisy that David experienced while living with sin (verses 16–19).

The psalm begins with an appeal to God's *khesed* ("lovingkindness"), which constitutes the basis for all forgiveness. Psalm 51:1 assembles three important characteristics of God. In addition to His *khesed*, there is "mercy" (*khanan*) and "compassion" (*rakhamim*). "All three form an integral part of *YHWH*'s canonical self-revelation in Exodus 34:6, and the psalmist is appealing to God to deal with him in accordance with His divine character."[6] There is a beautiful chiasm, using ritual terminology, that runs through the first section of the psalm (cf. Leviticus 13). It notes how divine forgiveness washes and cleanses us, leaving no trace of sin.[7] The chiasm of Psalm 51 centers on God's righteousness, which forms the legal base for forgiveness as He imputes His righteousness to the confessing sinner.

A *makhah* "blot out" (verse 1)
  B *kabas* "wash" (verse 2a)
    C *taher* "cleanse" (verse 2b)
      D *yada'* "I know" (verse 3)
        E *khata'* "I sinned" (verse 4a)
          F *tsadaq* "You may be found just" (verse 4c)

> E' *khata'* "sin" (verse 5)
> D' *yada'* "make me to know" (verse 6)
> C' *taher* "cleanse" (verse 7a)
> B' *kabas* "wash" (verse 7b)
> A' *makhah* "blot out" (verse 9)

The next section (verses 10–15) moves beyond forgiveness and describes the process of restoration in terms of Creation terminology. The Hebrew word *bara'* "create" is reserved exclusively for God's creative power and stands at the beginning of the Creation account (Genesis 1:1). As God created the world *ex nihilo*—out of nothing—He creates a new "clean heart" when we return to Him and gives us a "steadfast spirit"—a *ruakh nakon* ("a long-lasting breath") —pointing to divine grace's enduring change in us through justification and sanctification.

Anyone who has experienced the converting power of divine forgiveness has a story to tell, and David is no different. "Then I will teach transgressors Your ways, and sinners shall be converted to You" (Psalm 51:13). All of this ends with joyful praise (verses 14, 15). The psalm could end here, but the final verses of the poem consider the question of true worship and true sacrifice (verses 16–19).

It is somewhat disturbing that unconfessed sin in our life often leads us to be critical and judgmental of others. David's irate reaction to Nathan's parable vividly and sadly demonstrates this (2 Samuel 12:5, 6). We tend to rationalize our own failures by finding fault with others, which is the perfect definition of hypocrisy. In contrast, God is not looking for a "burnt offering" but for a "broken spirit . . . and a contrite heart" (Psalm 51:16, 17, ESV) and finds this in David's confession at the end of Nathan's speech (2 Samuel 12:13): "No sacrifice in the sacrificial system (Lev 1–7) could have atoned for David's premeditated sin of adultery and murder; only inward repentance, confession, and divine forgiveness could bring David back into harmony with God."[8]

Psalm 32 gives us two further glimpses into David's inner world after his sin with Bathsheba. The consequences of unconfessed sin in body, mind, and spirit should not be underestimated, and the old adage "confession is good for the soul" has its roots in the biblical text (James 5:16). David experienced the opposite effects during the time between his sin and confession: "When I kept silent, my bones grew old through my groaning all the day long" (Psalm 32:3). He loses his joie de vivre and feels hollow from within, his vitality draining away. Of course, we need to be careful not to fall into the trap of retribution theology, as Job's friends did. Physical, mental, or emotional suffering is not necessarily a sign of unconfessed sin, but in any case, the healing power of confession and the experience of God's *khesed* always holds true.

The end of Psalm 32 breaks into a joyful shout about God's grace, knowing that His *khesed* ("steadfast love") "surrounds the one who trusts in the LORD" (Psalm 32:10, 11, ESV). The one who has been forgiven has a story to tell and a new song to sing.

Pesher—Khesed in the Psalms

The Hebrew word *khesed* is one of the most meaningful words in the Old Testament. It appears 245 times in the Hebrew text, of which 127 occurrences are found in the book of Psalms. Its frequent use makes it a central theological term in the Psalter. The origin of the word is not easily traced, but it has been loosely connected with the Arabic root *hasada* ("band together for mutual aid"), and it is frequently connected to one of the divine names in the Psalms (e.g., *khesed YHWH*, the "steadfast love of the Lord"—Psalm 33:5). It can be translated with a variety of expressions that in essence reflect the dynamic character of God: *grace, love, steadfast love, loving-kindness, faithfulness, mercy.* These are the characteristics of Yahweh as the God of the covenant, and *khesed* in the Psalms is often used in the context of other covenant terms, such as *'emet* ("truth," e.g., Psalm 25:10) and *khanan* ("be gracious, merciful," e.g., Psalm 51:1). All three terms occur together in Exodus 34:6, the supreme self-revelation of God in the Old Testament. David experienced *khesed* after facing a clear death sentence for his adultery (cf. Leviticus 20:10) as God extended grace and forgiveness to him after he confessed his sin: "The LORD also has put away your sin; you shall not die" (2 Samuel 12:13).

Exodus 34:6 is one of the most frequently quoted or alluded to texts in the Old Testament, especially in Psalms (e.g., Psalms 31:19; 57:10; 86:5, 15; 91:4; 103:8–13; 108:4; 111:4, 8; 112:4; 116:5; 117:2; 138:2; 145:8; 146:6; etc.). It characterizes the God of the Old Testament as a God of grace, love, and mercy. God's *khesed* flows out into the human sphere, impacting human relationships when people show each other kindness. It even transcends ethnic boundaries (Ruth 1:8; 3:10), thus becoming an ethical norm for society (Proverbs 11:17).

In the Psalms, people who act out *khesed* are called *khasid* (25 times in Psalms), which is usually translated as the "godly ones" or even "saints," but the word really refers to those who show mercy and loving-kindness to others (Psalm 18:25). They are set apart by God and do not act in anger (Psalm 4:3, 4), they praise God (Psalm 30:4), they pray (Psalm 32:6), and they exhibit a self-sacrificial spirit (Psalm 79:2).

While the Hebrew word *khesed* is usually translated as *eleos* "mercy" in the Greek translation of the Old Testament, it has been connected to the Greek word *agape*, which in the New Testament refers to love as summing up God's nature (1 John 4:8, 16). This love (*agape*), as *khesed* in the Old Testament, is also connected to truth (*aletheia*) in the New Testament (2 Thessalonians 2:10). Thus, *khesed* can be understood as the existential summary of God's character. Biblical authors often draw on its depth of meaning, a meaning that was transferred into the New Testament word *agape*.

Edut—A student's moment of *khesed*

I always have a *khesed* moment in my Biblical Hebrew class, or rather, my students do. Biblical Hebrew is not the easiest language to learn because it involves a new writing system with an alphabet consisting of twenty-two consonants, as well as vowels that appear as points and symbols rather than individual letters. Other difficulties include adjusting to the opposite direction of writing (right to left) and the unfamiliar phonetics that are pronounced in the throat. In addition to this, students need to memorize vocabulary and learn paradigms—all with the purpose of reading the Old Testament in its original language. It is a rigorous task, and students spend three or four semesters studying Biblical Hebrew, but not always with rejoicing and singing of psalms.

I give weekly vocabulary quizzes that test the students' knowledge of new and previous vocabulary. Before the second or third quiz in the semester, I have a short worship at the beginning of class about the Hebrew word *khesed*, "mercy, grace, loving-kindness." I'm sure the students are thinking more about the upcoming quiz than the current worship, but during the quiz, I offer the students a *khesed* word. I take out my red pen and ask them to raise their hands if they want me to come to their desk and translate a word of their choice, a word they do not know. At first, they are skeptical, thinking it is a joke, and no one raises their hand. Then a desperate soul risks possible ridicule and accepts the offer. I go over to their quiz and write their *khesed* word in red pen, next to the Hebrew word they do not know. Soon, other hands go up, and quickly the whole class catches on. Students are thankful and will forever, in most cases, remember the Hebrew word I gave them. They also will not forget the meaning of *khesed*. As a matter of fact, students have come to me years after graduating, remembering their *khesed* word and the grace they received on the Hebrew vocabulary quiz.

Clearly, this is not on the scale of divine grace that David experienced when Nathan told him that God would also forgive him (2 Samuel 12:13), but life with God includes more than life-changing mercies that bring us back from the darkness and danger of unconfessed sin. It also includes the small daily graces that show us His faithfulness and enduring mercies. These aspects of faithfulness and steadfastness are part of the semantic depth of *khesed*. They highlight God's work in our lives and reflect the essence of His character shining through the sacred pages of Scripture, through the dark stories of sin, and through the psalmist's joyful choruses.

In the New Testament, this theme is also expressed in the Greek word *charis*, which means "grace." This term stands at the beginning of the last verse of Scripture, introducing the grand summary of God's love for humankind. "The grace of our Lord Jesus Christ be with you all. Amen." (Revelation 22:21)

Tehillim—Grace, grace, God's grace

Grace, grace, God's grace,
Grace that will pardon and cleanse within
Grace, grace, God's grace,
Grace that is greater than all our sin![9]

---

1. Richard Dawkins, *The God Delusion* (London: Bantam Press, 2006), 31.

2. Paul Copan and Matthew Flanagan, *Did God Really Command Genocide? Coming to Terms With the Justice of God* (Grand Rapids, MI: Baker Books, 2014), 9.

3. Dispensationalism, for example, understands most of the Old Testament as the dispensation of law versus the New Testament being the dispensation of grace.

4. Ángel Manuel Rodriguez, "God as Commander in Chief," Seventh-day Adventist Church Biblical Research Institute, accessed January 17, 2023, https://www.adventist biblicalresearch.org/materials/god-as-commander-in-chief/. See also Ellen G. White,

Patriarchs and Prophets (Mountain View, CA: Pacific Press®, 1958), 492.

5. The Hebrew text of 2 Samuel 11:4 seems to suggest that David took Bathsheba by force and that this was not necessarily a consensual act.

6. Martin G. Klingbeil, "Psalms 1–75," in *Seventh-day Adventist International Bible Commentary*, ed. Jacques Doukhan, vol. 6, *Psalms, Proverbs, Ecclesiastes, Song of Songs* (Nampa, ID: Pacific Press®, 2022), 223.

7. Klingbeil, 224.

8. Klingbeil, 225.

9. Julia H. Johnston, "Marvelous Grace" (Carol Stream, IL: Hope Publishing, 1938).

8

Wisdom for Righteous Living

If you live in the United States and there is an emergency, you know which number to call: 911. You depend on the wisdom of the dispatcher who answers the emergency call to quickly get you the appropriate help, be it law enforcement, medical services, the fire department, or a combination of all three. In the book of Psalms, these three digits also appear in a context of wisdom and law; one just needs to reverse their order: 119.

Ezra, most likely the final compiler and editor of the book of Psalms, arranged 3 of the 150 poems that deal with wisdom and law (Hebrew *torah*) in a way that readers could easily remember: Psalms 1, 19, and 119.[1] They are known as the three *torah* psalms, which also form part of the group of wisdom psalms (Psalms 1; 14; 19; 37; 73; 91; 112; 119; 128).[2] There is a close connection between wisdom and *Torah*, especially if one understands these terms within the context of the Old Testament.

Torah, in the modern Christian mindset, is often confined to the Ten Commandments because the Hebrew word *torah* is usually translated as "law" in the Old Testament. However, the Hebrew noun comes from the verb *yarah*, meaning "to teach, instruct," and refers to the sum of

God's instructions as found in the Scriptures. This is often likened to parental instruction, and the book of Proverbs, belonging to the so-called wisdom books of the Old Testament, uses the father-son relationship of instruction as a paradigm for wisdom. The Hebrew phrase *beni* ("my son") occurs twenty-two times in Proverbs, especially in the first seven chapters (Proverbs 1:8, 10, 15; 2:1; 3:1, 11, 21; 4:10, 20; 5:1, 20; 6:1, 3, 20; 7:1; 19:27; 23:15, 19, 26; 24:13, 21; 27:11; 31:2), and the paternal instruction leads to true wisdom:

> "Hear, *my son*, and receive my sayings,
> And the years of your life will be many.
> I have *taught* you in the way of *wisdom*;
> I have led you in right paths" (Proverbs 4:10, 11; emphasis added).

Biblical wisdom is not cognitive ability, and the corresponding Hebrew word *khokmah* "does not belong to the realm of theoretical knowledge or philosophy but rather refers to a proper understanding of the basic realities of life and God's dealings with humanity and the human role as moral agents."[3] Thus, biblical wisdom is making decisions based on divine fatherly instruction between morally right or wrong choices, between the "way of the righteous" and the "way of the ungodly" (Psalm 1:6).

Davar—Wisdom and Torah in Psalm 19

We tend to read the book of Psalms in a fragmented way, treating each individual poem as a separate unit that has no connection to the surrounding poems and even less of a connection to the overall structure of the Psalter. Since the 1990s, there has been an increased interest in reading the Psalms as a book[4] with macro-structural arrangements that run throughout, grouping psalms into meaningful units.

Psalm 19 finds itself at the center of one of those structures, a chiasm that spans Psalms 15–24. As noted in Chapter 2, a chiasm is a concentric step structure that creates a correspondence between each step as they move toward and away from the center. Coming from the Greek letter *chi* (X), a chiasm reflects this cross-like structure when diagrammed.

A Psalm 15: Question at the temple gate: "Who may abide?" (Psalm 15:1)
  B Psalm 16: God blesses His people: "You are . . . my cup" (Psalm 16:5)
    C Psalm 17: Praying for deliverance from enemies
      D Psalm 18: Royal psalm regarding battle
        E Psalm 19: Torah psalm: "The law . . . is perfect" (Psalm 19:7)
      D' Psalms 20; 21: Two royal psalms regarding battle
    C' Psalm 22: Praying for deliverance from enemies
  B' Psalm 23: God blesses His people: "My cup runs over" (Psalm 23:5)
A' Psalm 24: Question at the temple gate: "Who may ascend?" (Psalm 24:3)

It is interesting to note how the outer parts of the chiasm frame the idea of *torah* at the center: "Psalms 15–24 . . . are chiastically arranged around the second *torah* psalm (19) and demonstrate structurally how *torah* is embedded in worship (15; 24); divine blessing (16; 23); prayer (17; 22); and kingship (18; 20–21)."[5]

Psalm 19 can be divided into three parts moving from *general revelation* (Psalm 19:1–6) to *special revelation* (verses 7–11) and concluding with a *plea* for protection from presumptuous sins (verses 12–14). The theological term *general revelation* refers to what humankind can understand of God's character through nature, reasoning, and conscience. It begins with a praise of God as Creator (verses 1–3), alluding repeatedly to Genesis 1, and then focuses on the sun's daily journey through the sky, a motif that is familiar in the ancient Near East (verses 4–6). In Egyptian cosmology (figure 2), Nut, the goddess of heaven, supported by the air god Shu, arches over the earth god Geb, whose body is covered in vegetation. The sun-god Ra travels on a solar bark across the sky, shown twice to represent sunrise and sunset. Osiris, the god of the

Figure 2. Egyptian cosmology.

underworld, receives the setting sun. This demonstrates that looking at nature alone can lead to very different conclusions about God: "Apart from Christ we are still incapable of interpreting rightly the language of nature. The most difficult and humiliating lesson that man has to learn is his own inefficiency in depending upon human wisdom, and the sure failure of his efforts to read nature correctly. Of himself he cannot interpret nature without placing it above God."[6]

The pantheistic views (God is not above nature but the same as nature) of John Harvey Kellogg, a prominent figure in the early Seventh-day Adventist Church, represent a more recent misreading of natural revelation. Consequently, nature needs to be interpreted, and Psalm 19:7–11 moves from general to special revelation presenting *torah*, divine instruction, as the key to understanding our world and God. As a matter of fact, Psalm 19:4 already introduced this concept in the first section as "He has set a tabernacle for the sun," subjecting nature to God. "Interestingly, the divine name God only appears once in verses 1–6 and only in its shortened form (*'el*), whereas there is a sevenfold mention of *YHWH* in verses 7–14. Special revelation through God's Word points much more directly at God than natural revelation does."[7] Paul follows the same sequence from natural to special revelation in Romans 1; 2. Notably, he also quotes from another *torah* psalm (see Romans 1:16; Psalm 119:46).

The characteristics and consequences of *torah* are enumerated in a series of six synonyms ("law," "testimony," "statutes," "commandment," "fear of the Lord," and "judgments"): *torah* provides conversion, wisdom, enlightenment, and it endures forever. This is followed by a seventh summative statement (Psalm 19:10, 11), which compares *torah* with gold, yet not only ordinary but refined gold; and honey, yet not only the product but the source of the product, the honeycomb. The last consequence is the Law's preventive power as it warns us of oncoming danger. All of this means a rewarding life in the presence of God.

It is interesting to note that the poem's final section is a petition for protection from "presumptuous sins" (verses 12–14). We have seen above how a misreading of the natural world can lead us to place the creature above its Creator. In contrast, *torah* gives us wisdom and shows us our dependence on divine protection. It propels us into the arms of God, who instructs us and keeps us from falling. Then the "words of my mouth and the meditation of my heart" (verse 14) will be acceptable in God's "sight," just like the sacrifices offered in the sanctuary (cf. Leviticus 1:3).

Pesher—Two ways and a smitten rock

As Psalm 19:7 states, *torah* ("instruction") gives us the wisdom to choose the right way. From the beginning of the Psalter (Psalm 1:6) to its end (Psalm 146:8), we are reminded that there are only two ways, the way of the righteous and the way of the wicked. In Psalm 81, God expresses His yearning that Israel would finally "listen" (verses 5, 8 [twice], 11, 13) to what He has to say so that they "would walk in [His] ways" (verse 13). The usage of the Hebrew verb *shama'* "hear, listen" together with Israel in three verses (verses 8, 11, 13) recalls the famous *Shema Yisrael* of Deuteronomy 6:4 ("Hear, O Israel: The Lord our God, the

Lord is one!"), and this monotheistic confession serves as a reminder of the covenant between God and His people.

However, Israel did not always choose the right way. Psalm 81 recalls Israel's divine deliverance from Egypt during the Exodus (verses 5, 6) but then focuses on the story of Israel's failure at Meribah (verses 7–9). Through Israel's lack of trust in God's leading and their complaining about the lack of water at Meribah (Exodus 17:1–7), they failed God's test for them.[8] However, human failure was not met by divine abandonment but by marvelous grace, and the remainder of the psalm (Psalm 81:10–16) shows God's faithfulness to the covenant. Instead of only water, God will provide "honey from the rock" (verse 16), thus fulfilling one of the covenantal promises (Deuteronomy 8:8). "The psalm conveys the notion of salvation by God's grace because when the covenant is broken by disobedience, it can be renewed by the grace of God, so that the people can enjoy its blessings anew."[9]

There is one other aspect of grace in the story of the smitten rock, and it has to do with Moses' role as he faced the rock. Israel complaining of thirst in front of a rock occurred twice during the wilderness wanderings, once at the beginning of the Exodus at Meribah near Rephidim (Exodus 17:1–7), and then again, almost forty years later, at Meribah near Kadesh-barnea in Southern Palestine (Numbers 20:1–13). In both instances, Moses hit the rock and water gushed forth; however, only at Rephidim had God commanded Moses to strike the rock (Exodus 17:6). At Kadesh-barnea, God asked Moses to speak to the rock (Numbers 20:8), but Moses disobeyed and hit the rock a second time, an act that barred him from entering the Promised Land.

But grace can be found even in Moses' punishment: God still allowed water to come from the rock. In a culture in which honor and shame play a crucial role, God stood with His friend Moses and did not shame him in front of the people. But even more significant, after Moses hiked up Mount Nebo to take one last long look at the Promised Land, he saw more than is possible with the naked eye. God gave him a prophetic vision of salvation history as it would play out in the land beyond the Jordan: "He was permitted to look down the stream of time and behold the first advent of our Saviour."[10]

Edut—The life-saving value of *torah* and wisdom on a Swiss glacier

Natural revelation is spectacular when looking at the majestic beauty of the Swiss Alps. In 1988, on the first weekend in October, my brother and I decided to climb our first 4,000-meter peak. To be exact, this one is 4,151 meters (13,619 feet) above sea level. The Bishorn is in the Swiss canton of Valais, straight across from the iconic Weisshorn, and it is one of the easier peaks to climb for aspiring alpinists. We met on a Friday evening in the valley below and were joined by a Swiss-certified mountain guide who was also the father of a good friend.

After spending the night at a campsite and a short worship service on Sabbath morning, we began our ascent on Sabbath afternoon, reaching a mountain hut before sunset, the Cabane de Tracuit at 3,256 meters (10,682 feet), where we would spend the night. We would continue the ascent at four o'clock the next morning to make the summit by eight o'clock in the morning and still be able to descend all the way down into the valley by Sunday afternoon.

From the hut onward, it was glacier climbing all the way to the summit, and we were each equipped with a climbing harness, crampons, an ice axe, two climbing cords, carabiners, and a good amount of *torah* ("instruction"). Our mountain guide taught us how to use the equipment, and I specifically remember the instructions concerning the two shorter climbing cords that could be used as mechanical ascenders on a rope in case of a self-rescue from a glacier crevasse. Little did I know.

Early Sunday morning, we set off, with stars beautifully illuminating the glacier above us. It was cold, and the first snow had fallen, so the glacier was covered in a blanket of fresh snow, hiding any crevasses. We were roped up, with the mountain guide leading the way, my brother in the middle, and me at the end. It was a strenuous climb interrupted by our guide's careful prodding for potential crevasses with his ice axe before taking the next step. I felt the equipment was wearing me down, and as we climbed higher and the air got thinner, there were moments when I wanted to rest, but our guide relentlessly dragged us upward.

We made the summit as planned, somewhat exhausted from the lack of oxygen but happy to have conquered the mountain. On the descent, the wisdom of our guide dictated that the last person in the roped party would walk now in the front so that the guide could hold the group from behind, anchoring his ice axe if someone in front of him fell. So, I began to lead, carefully picking with my ice axe every step in front of me but somewhat uncertain as to what I was doing. Then my ice axe gave way as I prodded the snow in front of me. I extended my arm a bit further, and thinking I was feeling firm ground, I took a big step—into free-fall nothingness.

In an instant, I was dangling from my rope, swinging back and forth in a rather large crevasse. But our guide's wisdom and instruction had worked. Both he and my brother had rammed their ice axes into the ground, saving my fall. I was soon able to climb out the best I could, and they pulled me out of the crevasse completely. I was shaken but eternally thankful for the instruction received and the wisdom shared by our faithful mountain guide. Quoting God, Hosea put it like this: "I taught Ephraim to walk, taking them by their arms; . . . I drew them with gentle cords, with bands of love" (Hosea 11:3, 4). *Torah* and wisdom.

Tehillim—Cords of love

I've found a Friend; oh, such a Friend!

He loved me ere I knew Him;
He drew me with the cords of love,
And thus He bound me to Him.
And 'round my heart still closely twine
Those ties which nought can sever,
For I am His, and He is mine,
Forever and forever.[11]

---

1. Some commentators also include Psalm 111 among the *torah* psalms.

2. There are varying lists of wisdom psalms depending on the interpreter, but the list here is representative and focuses on the important didactic character of wisdom in the Old Testament. J. Clinton McCann, "The Psalms as Instruction," *Interpretation* 46, no. 2 (1992): 117–128.

3. Martin G. Klingbeil, "Introduction to Hebrew Poetry and Wisdom Books," in *Andrews Bible Commentary: Light. Depth. Truth.*, ed. Ángel Manuel Rodríguez (Berrien Springs, MI: Andrews University Press, 2020), 1:621.

4. Norman Whybray, *Reading the Psalms as a Book*, Supplements to *Vetus Testamentum*, vol. 222 (Sheffield: Sheffield Academic Press, 1996).

5. Martin G. Klingbeil, "Psalms 1-75," in *Seventh-day Adventist International Bible Commentary*, ed. Jacques Doukhan, vol. 6, *Psalms, Proverbs, Ecclesiastes, Song of Songs* (Nampa, ID: Pacific Press®, 2022), 18.

6. Ellen G. White, *Testimonies for the Church* (Mountain View, CA: Pacific Press®, 1948), 8:257.

7. Klingbeil, "Psalms 1-75," 108.

8. It is interesting that the psalmist portrays the incident at Meribah as God testing Israel (Psalm 81:7), while Moses describes it as Israel testing God (Exodus 17:2).

9. Dragoslava Santrac, "Psalms 76–150," in Doukhan, *International Bible Commentary*, 6:357.

10. Ellen G. White, *Patriarchs and Prophets* (Mountain View, CA: Pacific Press®, 1958), 475.

11. James G. Small, "I've Found a Friend" (1866).

9

Blessed Is He Who Comes in the Name of the Lord

Easter weekend at Southern Adventist University is special. On the Saturday before Easter Sunday, a walk-through pageant portrays the final days of Christ's ministry on earth, culminating with scenes of the Crucifixion and the Resurrection. The Passion play involves the whole university campus, beginning in the church with an introductory scene, then moving through a biblical animal zoo (with the odd llama in it), then into ancient Jerusalem, located along the central campus promenade. The setting is buzzing with stalls of peddlers, artisans, singing children, and other scenes that could represent the Holy City during Jesus' time.

On it goes to the Last Supper table, where Jesus solemnly washes His disciples' feet. Gethsemane plays out on an open lawn above the men's residence, and Christ's suffering becomes tangible as He sweats blood while battling the attacks of a menacing Satan. Pilate's palace is situated among the columns of Wright Hall, the central administration building on campus. From there, a flogged and sentenced Jesus is dragged through the middle of a mocking mob to Calvary, a small hill next to the running track. It gets quiet when Jesus breathes His last, and visitors walk slowly and pensively into the large gym to watch the Resurrection scene.

As many as ten thousand people visit campus on that Sabbath, guided through the pageant by a herald in groups of about six hundred to eight hundred people. My sons have been involved in the cast of more than five hundred students, faculty, and church members, playing mocking crowd bystanders at Pilate's palace or Roman soldiers with (an almost) true-to-reality heavy armor, or working the spotlight at the Resurrection scene.

Without fail, it has always been a rewarding experience. In spite of heavy armor and shivering cold snaps, my sons have always returned home quite happy, once again inspired by Christ's life, death, and resurrection.

As observers, our family has often walked through the Passion play and enjoyed the reaction of the people who come from the surrounding area to our campus. On one occasion, I remember walking through the Jerusalem marketplace behind a group of about twenty Arabic-speaking visitors. My Arabic is rather limited and based on a handful of words that I picked up while traveling and working in the Middle East, but there is one word that repeatedly came up, and it is a word I could clearly understand. As I listened to the animated conversation taking place in front of me, I heard the word *Isa*, the name used for Jesus in the Quran. Now, as far as I know, Arab Christians would usually use *Yasuʻ* as the name for Jesus based on the Hebrew *Yeshua*,[1] so it was not out of the question that the group I was following were Muslims who were attending Sonrise. They seemed to be discussing Jesus, whom they were getting to know as they followed Him through ancient Jerusalem on the campus of Southern Adventist University.

Davar—The Messiah foretold in the Psalms

The powerful scenes of Calvary are also present in the book of Psalms. Martin Luther once commented that the Psalter "should be precious and dear to us if only because it most clearly promises the death and resurrection of Christ, and describes His kingdom, and the nature and standing of all Christian people. It could well be called a 'little Bible' since it contains, set out in the briefest and most beautiful form, all that is to be found in the whole Bible."[2] It appears that the great German Reformer understood the coming of the Messiah to be a crucial and central theological theme in the book of Psalms, with the Psalter presenting a clear and detailed prophetic perspective of the coming of Jesus, the Christ.

However, since each psalm was written in a specific historical context, the question needs to be asked: What are the criteria to identify a Messianic prophecy in the Psalms? How do we determine whether the prophecy represents only a proclamation regarding an Old Testament personality, like an Israelite king? For example, the historical backdrop of Psalm 2 is a coronation of an Israelite king on Mount Zion, most likely David, during the tumultuous time of the united monarchy (Psalm 2:6). However, in the next verse, verse 7, we read a familiar statement that introduces messianic overtones, which are then reiterated in the New Testament and applied to Christ, the Messiah (cf. Hebrews 1:5): "The LORD has said to Me, 'You are My Son, today I have begotten You." Consequently, by moving beyond the immediate realities and elevating the language beyond the historical context and by being referenced under inspiration in the New Testament and applied to Christ, the Messianic character of Psalm 2 comes sharply into focus.

Furthermore, as Walter Kaiser, a distinguished evangelical Old Testament scholar, points out, the Old Testament authors were, for the most part, also aware of the prophetic significance of what God had inspired them to write: "The depictions of the coming Messiah should not be a random association of heterogeneous prognostications, arbitrarily introduced in the OT or haphazardly chosen to suit the purposes of the NT writers. Instead, they comprised one continuous plan of God, each being linked to an ongoing stream of announcements that continued to expand and grow as they moved forward in the progress of revelation."[3] He further suggests "that there are at least sixty-five direct, straightforward prophecies of the Messiah [in the Old Testament] that were meant to be apprehended (note: not comprehended) by the audiences to whom they were first addressed."[4]

In the following table, a selected list of messianic passages from the book of Psalms will be put side-by-side with their New Testament counterparts, accompanied by a short commentary[5] to highlight any important issues of interpretation. The list is not exhaustive but focuses on the passages that connect directly to Christ's life, death, and resurrection.[6]

OT Reference	Commentary	NT Reference
Psalm 2:7	Christ's divinity and sonship (see also Matthew 3:17; John 5:19-23, 25, 26; Acts 13:33; Hebrews 5:5), with the metaphor of God as Father, appear frequently in the psalms (e.g., Psalms 68:5; 89:26, 27).	Hebrews 1:5
Psalm 8:2	Jesus is quoting from the Greek translation of the Old Testament; thus, the slight variation between Old and New Testament references. God confounds the haughty through the helpless.	Matthew 21:15, 16
Psalm 8:6	The transferal of dominion recalls the Creation account of Genesis 1:26–28; the reference in Hebrews 2:8 transfers and extends this dominion irrevocably to Christ. Humanity is safe under Christ's dominion.	Hebrews 2:8
Psalm 16:10	Christ's resurrection from the grave (the untranslated Hebrew *sheol* is synonymous with "the grave") as a first fruit of victory over death provides the guarantee for all resurrections before and after Him (cf. Matthew 28:7).	Acts 2:27

OT Reference	Commentary	NT Reference
Psalm 22:1	Jesus quotes the verse verbatim in Aramaic. This text is the center of His seven sayings on the cross, expressing His feeling of abandonment as He breaks under the weight of the sins of this world. The psalm's language points beyond itself and connects to other messianic prophecies in the Old Testament.	Matthew 27:46
Psalm 22:7, 8	The dehumanization in derision plays out in this part of Psalm 22, pointing to the Messianic dimension of the poem. Christ is mocked on the cross by the crowd that questions His divinity, yet He ignores their challenge to prove Himself.	Luke 23:35
Psalm 22:15	Christ's thirst on the cross exemplifies the ebbing of His human strength and nearness of His approaching death (see also Psalm 69:21). He refuses the numbing bitter drink to preserve His senses in this most decisive moment of the great controversy (Matthew 27:34). Dry places in Scripture often wait to be rejuvenated by divine creative power (Psalm 107:35).	John 19:28
Psalm 22:16	The imagery is once more clearly Messianic, going far beyond the life circumstances of David. Christ's pierced hands and feet become the eternal signs of His saving commitment to humanity (Revelation 5:6), erasing any doubt about the reality of His sacrifice (John 20:27).	John 20:27
Psalm 22:18	The literal fulfillment of the dividing of Christ's clothes while he hung on the cross illustrates once more the prophetic accuracy with which Psalm 22 foreshadows Christ's suffering on the cross.	John 19:24

Psalms

OT Reference	Commentary	NT Reference
Psalm 31:5	Jesus appropriates these words on the cross, entrusting His "spirit" to God. Hebrew *ruakh* ("spirit, breath") refers to God's life-giving divine power as He breathes life into humans and retracts life at the point of death (Genesis 2:7).	Luke 23:46
Psalm 34:20	As the bones of the Passover lamb were not broken (Exodus 12:46), so the antitypical Lamb of God, suffering a terrible death, was also protected.	John 19:33
Psalm 41:9	David's betrayal by one of his closest friends and advisers, possibly Ahithophel (2 Samuel 15:31), points to Judas' betrayal of Jesus after the Last Supper. Eating together in the ancient Near East created strong bonds, exacerbating the ensuing betrayal even more.	Luke 22:47
Psalm 68:18	The image of a king's victory procession, returning from battle with his captives and treasures, is taken up by Paul in Ephesians 4:8 and applied to the ascension of Christ, who has conquered death and will take us home with Him.	Acts 1:9–11
Psalm 109:4	In the face of accusation, the psalmist turns to prayer, and Jesus, in His last moments, prays for His tormentors.	Luke 23:34
Psalm 109:8	In betraying Jesus and afterward hanging himself, Judas became a curse. When establishing the Christian church, the disciples replaced him with Matthias to complete the number of apostles.	Acts 1:20

OT Reference	Commentary	NT Reference
Psalm 110:4	Melchizedek, the Jebusite king-priest of Salem (Genesis 14:18–20), appears only here and again in the Epistle to the Hebrews. The lack of priestly attributions to King David emphasizes the Messianic intentions of the verse.	Hebrews 5:6
Psalm 118:22	The rejected stone becomes the "chief cornerstone" or "head of the corner" (Luke 20:17, RSV), which provides the foundational support for a building; the rejection of the Messiah is followed by His glorification as He is the foundation of a new living temple (see also Ephesians 2:20–22; 1 Peter 2:4–8).	Luke 20:17
Psalm 118:25, 26	All four Gospels include this psalm quotation. The initial shout of "Hosanna" as Jesus enters Jerusalem (Matthew 21:9, 15; Mark 11:9; Luke 19:38; John 12:13) reflects the Hebrew *hoshi'a na'* "please, save now!" This indicates urgency and not just jubilation. All of this is done "in the name of the Lord," which conveys submission and belonging.	Matthew 21:9

Pesher—Jesus and the book of Psalms

Jesus not only read the psalms but also quoted from them more than from any other book in the Old Testament (followed by the prophet Isaiah). This cemented the canonical status of the Psalter in the emerging Christian church. In the Sermon on the Mount, the elevation of the "meek" (Matthew 5:5) recalls Psalm 37:11. God's provisions for the "ravens" (Luke 12:24), and, by extension, for us, goes back to Psalm 147:9. "Away from me, you evildoers!" (Matthew 7:23, NIV), Jesus' words to those who follow Him only in word but not in deed at the end of time, are drawn from Psalm 6:8.

Toward the end of Christ's life, references to the Psalms became more frequent. There are nine quotations in the Passion story. After His triumphal entry to Jerusalem, He cries over the city that lost its "peace" (Luke 19:42), quoting from Psalm 122:7, 8 (Jesus follows the Greek Septuagint here), before he restores peace to the temple by cleansing it. Then praise, teaching, and healing return to its precincts (Luke 19:43–46; Matthew 21:12–14).[7]

And then there is Psalm 22, the poem that describes Christ's last moments in the most intense way, detailing the circumstances that accompanied the crucifixion scene (see above). Twice, Jesus utters words from the Psalms: from Psalm 31:5 (Luke 23:46) just before His death, and before that, the desperate cry of abandonment from the beginning of Psalm 22, a cry the Gospels record in Aramaic, the spoken language in Jesus' day, followed by the translation: "And about the ninth hour Jesus cried out with a loud voice, saying, 'Eli, Eli, lama sabachthani?' that is, 'My God, My God, why have You forsaken Me?' " (Matthew 27:46).

As he often did during His life, Jesus returns to the Psalms to find comfort and to connect the prophetic dots that have pointed to Him since the time of King David (Luke 24:44). Psalm 22 is replete with these pointers, and the mocking leaders of Israel, just hours before, had quoted from the same psalm, thus unwittingly highlighting its messianic significance (Matthew 27:43; cf. Psalm 22:7, 8). Jesus died before He could recite the whole of Psalm 22, but His quote of the initial line serves as a challenge for us to complete the recitation of the poem in its entirety to tell the good news of Christ's death and resurrection, as long as history lasts: "The reciting must go on, because the story has to be retold 'to the next generation' (Ps. 22:30; see also Ps. 102:18). Everyone needs to hear that 'He has done this' (Ps. 22:31)."[8]

Edut—**Arise, my love**

The final resurrection scene of Sonrise at Southern Adventist University is an impressive experience:[9] a tranquil garden tomb guarded by weary Roman soldiers turns into a battlefield between Gabriel, who has been sent to call the Savior forth from the grave, and Satan, who is defending Christ's dead body against the heavenly life-giving messenger. To the lyrics of the song "Arise, My Love" (Eddie Carswell), the epic battle plays out in front of the stone-secured grave. Satan is finally defeated by Gabriel and thrown into a "lake" of fire integrated into the stage, accompanied by a loud explosion and a host of fireworks. Like a pebble, the stone rolls back, and Jesus comes forth. The scene presents a glorious climax as redemption is accomplished.

At first, we were a bit hesitant to watch the scene with our youngest son, Matthias, as we were not quite sure how he would react to the commotion, explosions, and pyrotechnics. He was about six years old when we took him for the first time. He was sitting on my lap, and I was ready to cover his ears when it came time for Satan to be overcome and thrown into the fire pit. But I was too late, and the explosion came. I will never forget my son's spontaneous reaction as evil was conquered and Christ arose. He threw up his little arms and shouted at the top of his lungs, "Yes," cheering Gabriel on. Pure joy. At that moment, resurrection became an exuberant reality for him. It still is.

Tehillim—**He is risen today**

The Cross is empty
Discarded and rotting away
Sabbath brings rest
Evil triumphant—it seems.
The Tomb is empty
Vacated and full of fresh air

Psalms

My heart is full—thankful as I sing
"Christ the Lord is risen today."
King David says: I told you so
When we meet on final resurrection-day
And we smile, both redeemed.
　　—Martin G. Klingbeil

1. There is some debate about the appropriateness of using *Isa* in Arab Christian circles as the *Isa* of the Quran is quite distinct from the New Testament Jesus of Nazareth, the Son of God and Messiah. See Ayman S. Ibrahim, "Should Christians Use the Quranic Name of Jesus in Arabic Bible Translations?" *Jenkins Center for the Christian Understanding of Islam, The Southern Baptist Theological Seminary*, January 24, 2023, https://jenkins.sbts.edu/2021/07/15/should-christians-use-the-quranic-name-of-jesus-in-arabic-bible-translations/.

2. Martin Luther, *Martin Luther: Selections From His Writings*, ed. John Dillenberger (New York: Random House, 1962), 38.

3. Walter C. Kaiser Jr., "Biblical Theology and the Interpretation of Messianic Texts," *Andrews University Seminary Studies* 34, no. 2 (Autumn 1996): 208, https://digitalcommons.andrews.edu/cgi/viewcontent.cgi?article=2253&context=auss.

4. Kaiser, 208.

5. The commentaries are based on Martin G. Klingbeil, "Psalms 1–75," in *Seventh-day Adventist International Bible Commentary*, ed. Jacques Doukhan, vol. 6, *Psalms, Proverbs, Ecclesiastes, Song of Songs* (Nampa, ID: Pacific Press®, 2022), 37–311; Dragoslava Santrac, "Psalms 76–150," in Doukhan, *International Bible Commentary*, 6:313–680.

6. Some websites list more than 90 Messianic prophecies in the book of Psalms (e.g., https://www.shalach.org/PropheciesTable/prophecieslst1.htm). The following are usually identified as the main group of Messianic psalms: Psalms 2; 8; 16; 22; 34; 40; 41; 45; 68; 69; 72; 109; 110; and 118. See Walter C. Kaiser, *The Messiah in the Old Testament* (Grand Rapids, MI: Zondervan, 1995).

7. William L. Holladay, *The Psalms Through Three Thousand Years: Prayerbook of a Cloud of Witnesses* (Minneapolis, MN: Fortress Press, 1996), 115–119.

8. Marcos Paseggi, "A Poem in Progress," *Adventist Review*, March 28, 2013, 277.

9. An amateur video of the Sonrise Resurrection scene can be found at https://www.youtube.com/watch?v=JVcTZlg1DPU beginning at 10:20.

10

Lessons of the Past

Some of our stories define us and become pillars of our faith journey. The following is one of those. It was a dark and stormy night. The wind had been howling, whipping the clouds into a blizzard. Snow had been falling throughout the night, covering the countryside with a thick white blanket. In the morning, after the stormy night had passed, I and some classmates sat down to an early breakfast in the cafeteria of Seminar Schloss Bogenhofen, the Adventist college in Austria. It was the winter of 1986, and I was in my first year of studying theology. Soon after the beginning of the school year, we had formed a quartet and enjoyed singing together. Today we were excused from all classes because the school administration had requested that we represent the school at a funeral two hours' drive away. An elderly lady had passed away, and one of her sisters, who was the only Adventist in the family, had asked Bogenhofen to send somebody to sing.

Right after breakfast, we set off to the little village where the funeral was to take place, a two-hour drive over country roads and through a mountain pass. After the heavy snowfall, the roads were barely passable, and thirty minutes into the trip, the engine oil-pressure indicator suddenly started flashing. We stopped, checked underneath the car, and sure enough, black oil was dripping onto the white snow. We looked up, and there was a gas station with a repair shop not more than fifty yards ahead of us. The first sign of divine providence: On country roads in Austria, gas stations with repair shops are the exception, not the rule. God had timed the breakdown well!

We pushed the car into the station, and the mechanic assessed the damage. He told us that the car could be repaired for about $200. I was shocked—this was a lot of money for a poor theology student, and I had no idea how we would pay the bill. Yet, there we were, broken down but still needing to sing at the funeral.

As we were wondering whether this was the end of our trip that day, the mechanic reviewed our car papers, and noted that we had an auto club membership and were eligible for a rental car for the duration of the repair. This was the second sign of divine providence: a gas station on a country road in Austria with a repair shop *and* a rental car station.

We were soon on the road again, now in a rental car heading toward the mountain pass. The pass was open, but as we were winding up and down the mountains, the car suddenly slid across the snow-covered road, and after a full 180-degree spin, we found ourselves at a bus stop across the road facing the opposite direction, as if parked by an angel. This was the third sign of divine providence: on mountain passes in Austria, there are few bus stops, and God had timed the incident once more so well that at the precise moment we spun across the road, there was no oncoming traffic. We realized now that the enemy was hard at work to prevent us from singing at the funeral. We paused, bowed our heads, and prayed. Earlier, we had asked for traveling mercies, but now our prayers were heartfelt and existential, asking the God of history to take charge of our personal history that day.

Lessons of the Past

Davar—God in history

Psalm 78, with seventy-two verses, is the second-longest poem (after Psalm 119) in the book of Psalms. It belongs to a group of historical psalms that review God's deeds in history (Psalms 77; 78; 105; 106; 135; 136). Its epic dimensions contribute to the argument it creates: God has led His people in the past, and He will continue to lead them in the future, especially the descendants of King David (Judah), unless they rebel as the tribe of Ephraim (Israel) did. Ultimately, God wants us to learn the lessons of the past; some are glorious, and others are painful. This leads us to the somewhat enigmatic superscription of the psalm: It is a *maskil*, an often untranslated Hebrew term (e.g., ESV), that appears thirteen times in psalm titles (Psalms 32; 42; 44; 45; 52; 53; 54; 55; 74; 78; 88; 89; 142). Based on the verb *sakal* ("to instruct"), it could be rendered as an "instructive poem." In Psalm 14:2, the same word (*maskil*) is used to describe "one who understands," a "wise person," who is then contrasted with *nabal*, "a fool" who claims that "there is no God" (verse 1). True wisdom learns from the past and follows God's instructions for the present.[1] Twice Psalm 78 moves from Egypt to Canaan (verses 12–39—Exodus and wilderness wanderings; verses 40–72—ten plagues and conquest), with both movements describing God's wondrous historical deeds contrasted with staggering human rebellion, and ultimately ending with God's mercy and grace (verses 33–39; 65–72).[2]

Psalm 78:1–8 invites its readers to listen to *torah* ("law, instruction"), just as Deuteronomy 6:7 encouraged the ancient Israelites on the threshold to the Promised Land to "instruct" their children so that they would not forget to "love the Lord your God with all your heart" verse 5) and remember His wondrous deeds. We often reduce *Torah* to the Ten Commandments or the Pentateuch, but it really is the sum of all the divine instruction found in the Old Testament (John 15:25). Remembrance serves as a powerful antidote to rebellion. Ephraim's failure (Psalm 78:9–11) to remember God's law demonstrates what happens if rebellion continues.

The defiant tribe turned on God and led Israel (the northern tribes) into sin. Two hundred years later, in 722 BC, they were conquered by the Assyrians and taken into captivity.

The history of Old Testament Israel is an up-and-down contrast between "God's wondrous deeds [and] Israel's repeated rebellion."[3] Correspondingly, Psalm 78 moves back and forth between devotion to God and apostasy.

The Exodus from Egypt and the rebellion of Israel in the wilderness are juxtaposed with each other in verses 12–32. Although God divided the Red Sea, provided a cloud by day and a fire by night, and supplied gushing water from the rock and manna from heaven, they still rebelled and "turned back to Egypt" (Acts 7:39). They had left Egypt physically but were still living there spiritually.

Yet, grace and mercy prevail. At the end of the first movement of the Psalm, God is described as a "compassionate" God who "atoned for their iniquity" (Psalm 78:38, ESV; cf. Exodus 34:6; Daniel 9:24). The Hebrew verb *zakar* ("to remember") plays an important role in this section: "First, they remembered that God was their Rock (v. 35), then God remembered that they were but flesh (v. 39), and finally they forgot [lit. 'they did not remember'] His power (v. 42) and returned to their own ways."[4] When we remember, we repent and return to God. When God remembers, He saves. When we forget (or, rather, do not remember), we turn our backs on Him. But God is not like us. He always remembers; He never forgets.

In combatting Israel's forgetfulness, the psalmist once more returns to the events of the Exodus and, more specifically, to God's miraculous deliverance through the ten plagues (Psalm 78:40–55). Yet, as during the wilderness wanderings, rebellion once more surfaced during Israel's conquest of Canaan (ca. 1400–1050 BC). This led God to eventually abandon His sanctuary at Shiloh, where the ark had been housed for almost three hundred years, recalling the capture of the ark by the Philistines during Eli's priesthood (verses 60, 61; cf. 1 Samuel 4:1–7:2).

The end of Shiloh, also recorded in Jeremiah 7:12–14 and 26:6, provides the transition to the final part of the psalm, which focuses on David's election as king over Israel. It was David who brought the ark of the covenant to Jerusalem from Kirjath Jearim, where it had been for twenty years after the Philistines had returned it to Israel (1 Samuel 4–7). David shepherded the ark and Israel (Psalm 78:70, 71), just as the Divine Shepherd had shepherded Israel in the wilderness (verse 52).

Psalm 78 speaks to the importance of remembering how God has led His people in the past. However, it is not a perfect past but a true depiction of human forgetfulness and divine remembrance. God's mighty deeds are painted in broad strokes on the canvas of tumultuous human history as it converges with the redeeming graces of salvation history.

Pesher—Historical pillars of faith

The historicity of biblical events has come under attack during the last two centuries. With the introduction of historical criticism (also known as the historical-critical method or higher criticism) during the nineteenth century, the historical veracity of Scripture was questioned. Based on the philosophical presuppositions of correlation (no supernatural intervention in history), analogy (present experience determines the probabilities of past events), and criticism (there are no absolutes or truth, only probabilities), the divine revelation and the inspiration of the Bible was negated, which led to a reading of Scripture as a collection of ancient documents and not as the Word of God. Thus, the fundamental historical acts of divine intervention throughout the history of ancient Israel are reduced to insignificant events or legends that were embellished by later editors and redactors of the biblical text.[5]

In this paradigm, Moses never wrote the Pentateuch; it was written by several unknown authors over five centuries. Daniel did not write his book either. And Isaiah? At best, he wrote only the first thirty-nine chapters of his book. Biblical prophecies, to the historical critic, are just *vaticinia ex eventu* (prophecies written *after* the event), thus rendering God a sociological construct of the priestly classes who sought to secure their ideological hold on the masses through cult and religion.

However, a close reading of the Psalter reveals that the authors of the psalms considered God's "wondrous deeds" in history as accurate historical events to which they would return to make sense of their present historical situations. This becomes all the more significant as the book of Psalms, written over a period of about a thousand years, sometimes parallels the historical events it references.

There are five historical events that the psalmists return to with regularity, making them the pillars of biblical historicity: Creation (Psalms 8; 19; 33; 65; 73; 74; 89; 90; 92; 96; 100; 104; 113; 115; 119; 121; 139; 146; 147; 148),[6] the time of the patriarchs (Psalms 14; 20; 24; 47; 53; 59; 78; 79; 99; 135; 105; 106; 147),[7] the Exodus from Egypt (Psalms 17; 18; 20; 34; 46; 47; 60; 66; 68; 76; 78; 105; 106; 135; 136),[8] the conquest of the Promised Land (Psalms 16; 24; 44; 47; 60; 66; 68; 78; 105; 106; 135; 136; 149),[9] and the reign of King David (Psalms 18; 20; 21; 45; 72; 84–89; 110; 132; 144).[10] Denial of the historicity of these events and individuals undermines the truth about origins, the Sabbath, the sanctuary, salvation, resurrection, eschatology, and ultimately, faith in Jesus Christ, the Messiah.

Edut—An elderly lady's note

We arrived at the funeral just in time and squeezed into the little cemetery chapel, just ahead of the congregation. It was cold, and we climbed the steep staircase to the balcony from which we were supposed to sing. Austrian cemetery chapels usually date back hundreds of years and have excellent acoustics. Beautiful harmonies filled the room as we sang an old hymn composed in 1657 by Georg Neumark ("If You but Trust in God to Guide You"), who wrote about God's wondrous deeds and provisions while experiencing the atrocities of the Thirty Years' War (1618–1648).

Lessons of the Past

When the funeral was over and the last harmony had echoed away, people began to stir below, and we got ready to leave. Cold and hungry but nonetheless happy, we descended the staircase to greet the people. As we mingled, I happened to meet the elderly Adventist lady who had requested our presence. Her eyes were brimming with tears, and she spoke softly, telling me how meaningful our songs had been to her and her family, how she believed that our music had comforted people and given them renewed hope for the resurrection at Christ's return.

As she was shaking my hand, I suddenly felt a piece of paper in my hand. Then she turned and disappeared among the other people. Another person came up to thank me, and I absent-mindedly put the paper into my coat pocket. Finally, we headed for the car to start the return journey. As we rode along, we recounted the blessings of the morning and how God had used us to be a blessing to others—and most of all, how He had brought us safely to our destination against all attempts by the adversary to derail our mission.

With that, the worry about our broken car returned, and we began to wonder how we would pay for the engine repair. Then I remembered the piece of paper in my pocket, and I thought I would share the note I had received in the church. I put my hand inside my coat and pulled it out. And here was the last sign of divine providence. To my surprise, it was not a piece of paper; it was two pieces of paper, the equivalent of $200, folded nicely together. It was the exact amount we needed for the repair.

God's mighty deeds throughout the history of the Old Testament, from Creation to the time of the patriarchs, from the Exodus to the conquest, and to the reign of King David, stand alongside His mighty deeds in my life on that cold Austrian morning long ago: "We have nothing to fear for the future, except as we shall forget the way the Lord has led us, and His teaching in our past history."[11] I'm certain that you, too, have a story to tell, a tale of God's mighty deeds in your life that have become your own pillars of faith.

Psalms

Tehillim—"If You But Trust in God to Guide You"

If you but trust in God to guide you
And place your confidence in Him,
You'll find Him always there beside you,
To give you hope and strength within.
For those who trust God's changeless love
Build on the rock that will not move.[12]

---

1. Martin G. Klingbeil, "Psalms 1–75," in *Seventh-day Adventist International Bible Commentary*, ed. Jacques Doukhan, vol. 6, *Psalms, Proverbs, Ecclesiastes, Song of Songs* (Nampa, ID: Pacific Press®, 2022), 88.

2. Dragoslava Santrac, "Psalms 76–150," in Doukhan, *International Bible Commentary*, 6:333.

3. Martin G. Klingbeil, "Psalms," in *Andrews Bible Commentary. Light. Depth. Truth.*, ed. Ángel Manuel Rodríguez (Berrien Springs, MI: Andrews University Press, 2020), 1:713.

4. Klingbeil, "Psalms 1–75," 713.

5. Gerald A. Klingbeil, "Historical Criticism," *Dictionary of the Old Testament: Pentateuch*, ed. T. Desmond Alexander and David W. Baker (Downers Grove, IL: InterVarsity Press, 2003), 401–420.

6. Alexej Muráň, "The Creation Theme in Selected Psalms," in *The Genesis Creation Account and Its Reverberations in the Old Testament*, ed. Gerald A. Klingbeil (Berrien Springs, MI: Andrews University Press, 2015), 189–223.

7. Abraham Gosse, "Abraham and David," *Journal for the Study of the Old Testament* 34, no. 1 (2009): 25–31.

8. Daniel J. Estes, "The Psalms, the Exodus, and Israel's Worship," in *Reverberations of the Exodus in Scripture*, ed. R. Michael Fox (Eugene, OR: Pickwick, 2014), 35–50.

9. Judith Gärtner, "The Historical Psalms: A Study of Psalms 78, 105, 106, 135 and 136 as Key Hermeneutical Texts in the Psalter," *Hebrew Bible and Ancient Israel* 4, no. 4 (2015): 373–399.

10. Robert E. Wallace, "The Narrative Effect of Psalms 84–89," *Journal of Hebrew Scriptures* 11, no. 10 (2011), http://dx.doi.org/10.5508/jhs.2011.v11.a10.

11. Ellen G. White, *Life Sketches of Ellen G. White* (Mountain View, CA: Pacific Press®, 1943), 196.

12. Georg Neumark, "If You but Suffer God to Guide You" (1641).

11

Longing for God in Zion

For several days, we had been laboriously excavating a large 2,700-year-old destruction layer at Lachish. After Jerusalem, it is the second most important city during much of the Old Testament period. It was the 2014 archaeological excavation season conducted by Southern Adventist University and The Hebrew University of Jerusalem, and we were digging with about 120 volunteers and staff in southern Israel.

We excavated the dramatic remains of the Assyrian attack on Lachish in 701 BC, when Sennacherib (705–681 BC) systematically destroyed the cities of ancient Judah—yet stopped short of conquering Jerusalem because the Angel of the Lord killed 185,000 Assyrians and saved King Hezekiah and his people from certain disaster (2 Kings 18; 19; Isaiah 36; 37).[1] In the destruction debris, we came across a fully intact dipper juglet, a small vessel that was used in biblical times to scoop liquids from larger storage vessels. Such juglets could also be used to store silver, jewelry, or other precious objects. As we carefully sifted through the ancient sediment in and around the dipper juglet, we came across four clay seal impressions the size of a thumbnail, so-called bullae, used to seal documents.

The owner of the juglet, evidently a high official at Lachish, who had received sealed documents from Jerusalem, carefully detached the seal impressions as proof of receipt, and stored the important objects in the dipper juglet. Two of them were identical and came from the same seal bearing a Hebrew inscription that read "Belonging to Eliakim, son/descendent of Yehuzerach." This notation connected them to a royal steward with the same name who was over the household of King Hezekiah in Jerusalem (2 Kings 18:17–19).[2]

Figure 3. Drawing of seal impression from Tel Lachish with two grazing does (Credit: *The Fourth Expedition to Lachish 2013–2017*)

It was a fascinating find that directly relates the biblical text to the archaeological object. Even more intriguing was the fact that all four seal impressions found inside the juglet bore the same image, the so-called "grazing doe" motif depicting a deer (or two deer facing each other) with its head lowered to the ground, searching for water and food. Seals of court officials from other excavations dated to the time of Hezekiah show the same image, almost as if Judah's king wanted to use a highly biblical and spiritual imagery not associated with any pagan deities. It would serve as a type of royal brand, creating a national identity of longing for and trusting in God's saving presence more than human alliances (Isaiah 30:1–5). This would be a distinct marker during times of warfare against an overpowering enemy. Much like their modern counterparts, the ancient Assyrians knew very well how to wage media warfare, as the famous Lachish reliefs attest. Sennacherib commissioned and installed the reliefs in his throne room in Nineveh after he had to withdraw from Jerusalem.[3]

Davar—As the deer pants for the waters

Psalm 42:1 seems to have been immortalized in the images found on these seals and seal impressions: "As the deer pants for the water brooks, so pants my soul for You, O God." They express an intense longing for

God's presence through imagery that evokes a dry and parched landscape through which a lonely deer is wandering in its search for water and food.

The Hebrew word *nepesh*, translated as "soul" at the end of Psalms 42:1 and the beginning of verse 2, refers to the whole being, not to a separate entity apart from the body. In the OT, "soul" refers to the whole person, a living and complete being as created by God (Genesis 2:7), even extending to the nature of animals (verse 19). It is God's breath that brings life, and the primary meaning of *nepesh* refers to the "throat"—the part of the body where breathing, drinking, and eating occur (Numbers 21:5). The mistranslation "soul" for this word in most modern Bible translations has been heavily influenced by Greek dualism imported into early Christianity.[4]

The image of the panting deer represents an existentially threatening situation for the animal, which makes sense in the semi-arid climate of Old Testament Israel. However, the psalmist's longing for water goes far beyond the life-giving liquid. In the second part of the psalm, water is abundant and rushing down in waterfalls from Mount Hermon in northern Israel, recalling the cascades at Baniyas, near Tel Dan, the New Testament Caesarea Philippi (Psalm 42:6, 7). But here, it is not lack of water that is life-threatening; it is the "waves and billows [that] have gone over me" (Psalm 42:7; cf. Jonah 2:3). Based on this northern geography, scholars have suggested that the psalmist was removed from Jerusalem by circumstances beyond his control, longing to return (e.g., David fleeing from his son Absalom). However, the panting deer and the threatening waters are only images of the psalmist's longing for God, a longing that is satisfied in a specific place.

The language of Psalm 42 identifies this place. The passage is replete with references to the sanctuary and the psalmist's longing for an encounter with Yahweh. He wants "to appear before God" (verse 3), an expression that immediately associates the poem with the yearly feasts at the sanctuary (Deuteronomy 16:16; 1 Samuel 1:22). He recalls the processions "to the house of God" during a "pilgrim feast" (Psalm 42:4). The "countenance" (Hebrew *paneh* "face") that is referred to in the twice-repeated refrain[5] is first "His countenance" (Psalm 42:5) and then becomes "my countenance" (verse 11; cf. Psalm 43:5), recalling how an encounter with God changes and transforms us, something that Moses experienced when he came down from Mount Sinai (Exodus 34:29–35). The search for God's face (Hebrew *paneh*, frequently translated as "presence"—e.g., Psalm 41:12) is ultimately the desire to find God in His sanctuary, and Psalm 63 uses the same imagery of thirst in a parched land with a longing for being in God's sanctuary:[6]

> O God, you are my God; earnestly I seek you;
>   my soul thirsts for you;
> my flesh faints for you,
>   as in a dry and weary land where there is no water.
> So I have looked upon you in the sanctuary,
>   beholding your power and glory (Psalm 63:1, 2, ESV).

As a matter of fact, the psalmists seem to repeatedly gravitate to the sanctuary.[7]

Pesher—The sanctuary as the center of gravity in the Psalms

When King Nebuchadnezzar destroyed the Solomonic temple in 586 BC, the inhabitants of Jerusalem who had survived the Babylonian onslaught watched in horror as the flames consumed the precious building. It had been the center of the Jewish religion and economy, and the dwelling place of Yahweh. It was a turn of events once thought impossible. The Judahites had come to consider the temple as a guarantor of their survival. It had become a talisman or lucky charm, causing Jeremiah to repeatedly warn the Jews not to trust in a building but to trust in God: "Do not trust in these deceptive words: 'This is the Temple of the LORD, the temple of the LORD, the temple of the LORD' " (Jeremiah 7:4, ESV). In the end, all that remained of the once-glorious building was charred wood and rubble (2 Kings 25; 2 Chronicles 36; Jeremiah 52).

Interestingly, the center of the psalms focuses on the theme of the sanctuary, describing the capture of Jerusalem and the destruction of the temple by the Babylonian army in graphic detail: there are axes and hammers, a raging fire, the breaking down of walls and wooden structures, and ultimately, complete destruction (Psalm 74:1–11). The pain of the psalmist and the Jewish community raises two questions that surface in every era of human history: "Why?" (verse 11) and "How long?" (verse 10).

The first question is the question of theodicy (God's righteousness in the face of evil and human suffering), and it finds an answer in the preceding psalm, Psalm 73. The author of this poem finds an answer as to why the righteous suffer while the wicked prosper (verses 2–16) only when he enters the sanctuary: "Until I went into the sanctuary of God; then I understood their end" (verse 17). Interestingly, this verse is also located at the center of the poem, and it resolves the big question of "why" both theologically and geographically. God will restore justice and righteousness at the appropriate time, and human suffering can result in a more intimate knowledge of God's mercy and love (Job 42:5). God's presence in the sanctuary brings the puzzle pieces together—finally.

The second question ("How long?") finds its answer in Psalm 75. Here, God is described as a judge who will bring justice and end the suffering of His people at the "proper time" (verse 2). Then all wrongs will be righted because God will "cut off" the "horns of the wicked" (verse 10). The cutting off of the horns is also associated with sanctuary imagery, as the altar in the temple had horns projecting from each of its four corners (Exodus 27:2). The horns could be taken hold of as a request for asylum (1 Kings 1:50–53) or cut off in order to desecrate the altar in cases of idolatry (Amos 3:14). Thus, the structural center of the Psalter, Psalms 73–75, is focused on the sanctuary, and serves as its theological center.[8]

It's been said that "a frame makes the painting." We learned this when we acquired a watercolor painting from an artist friend for a modest price and then looked for a suitable frame. To our surprise, it turned out that the frame was more expensive than the painting. In art, the frame and painting must work with each other; they enhance each other.

In the same way, a close look at the beginning and end of the psalter reveals a frame that enhances the theological focus point of its center. The righteous in Psalm 1:3 is likened to "a tree planted by the rivers of water," which clearly connects to sanctuary imagery. In various texts throughout the Old Testament, the righteous are described as being planted in the precincts of the temple (Exodus 15:17; Psalm 46:4; 65:4; 92:12–14; Jeremiah 17:7–13; Ezekiel 47:12). Likewise, the final symphony of praise at the end of the Psalms originates in the sanctuary (verse 1b), or more specifically, in the heavenly sanctuary, located in "His mighty firmament" (verse 1c).[9] References to the sanctuary permeate the book of Psalms from its beginning, through its midpoint, and to its end—thus demonstrating how the sanctuary tells the story of salvation. It clearly points to Christ's sacrifice and His work of atonement from beginning to end.

Edut—Thinking about church

The temple in ancient Israel served as the epicenter for a community of faith. Theologically, it revealed and foreshadowed the Messiah wherever one looked. It was also a physical place where prayers were answered (Psalm 5), doubts were addressed (Psalm 73), justice was meted out (Psalm 11), yearly feasts were celebrated (Psalms 120–134), and God was encountered (Psalm 63). In short, it was the place where faith was lived out daily.

Longing for God in Zion

Today, the sanctuary message remains close to the theological center of the Seventh-day Adventist Church, firmly intertwined with its origins, integral to its beliefs, and crucial for its understanding of eschatology. But at times, it seems to be relegated to an out-of-date set of Bible studies, or to a one-evening topic in a full-scale evangelistic series, or maybe the distinguishing mark that sets us apart from evangelical Christianity. Nevertheless, it is an important theological anchor for a church living through the end times, an "anchor of the soul, a hope that enters into the inner place behind the curtain" (Hebrews 6:19, ESV).

For the psalmists, however, it represented so much more, and their longing for it was existential. But beyond the theological insights it brings, how does it impact our view of church and our physical sanctuary, particularly after COVID? Many churches have shifted to an online presence because large gatherings have been problematic. It seems that community has been lost, the church has been scattered, and "church has changed."[10]

However, we have also rediscovered the value of community in small groups and house churches, and outdoor churches as well. We have experienced new opportunities and the blessings of mutual and tangible support in times of physical and financial hardship. We have renewed appreciation for the simple beauty of a hymn being sung after months of listening or humming only. We sense the therapeutic benefits of a human touch after long periods of isolation, social distancing, and loneliness. Maybe post-COVID life provides us with an opportunity to understand church as a sanctuary in times of distress, built not on the premise of "bigger is better" but on the mission of drawing people into the presence of God and back to the sanctuary. That is what the psalmists longed for throughout the book of Psalms, and that is what we long for as well.

Psalms

Tehillim—Song of a deer

As the deer panteth for the water
So my soul longeth after Thee
You alone are my heart's desire
And I long to worship Thee [11]

---

1. For a preliminary report of the 2013–2017 excavations at Lachish, see Yosef Garfinkel, Michael G. Hasel, Martin G. Klingbeil, Igor Kreimerman, Michael Pytlik, Jon W. Carroll, Jonathan W. B. Waybright, Hoo-Goo Kang, Gwanghyun Choi, SangYeup Chang, Soonhwa Hong, Arlette David, Itamar Weissbein, and Noam Silverberg, "The Canaanite and Judean Cities of Lachish, Israel: Preliminary Report of the Fourth Expedition, 2013–2017," *American Journal of Archaeology* 125, no. 3 (2021): 419–459, http://doi.org/10.3764/aja.125.3.0419.

2. Martin G. Klingbeil, Yosef Garfinkel, Michael G. Hasel, and Nestor Petruk, "Four Judean Bullae from the 2014 Season at Tel Lachish," *Bulletin of the American Schools of Oriental Research* 381 (2019): 41–56, http://doi.org/10.1086/703122.

3. The Lachish reliefs are bas-relief panels that show the Assyrian onslaught on Lachish in graphic images. They are now housed in the British Museum in London. For more information and a virtual tour of the reliefs, see "Assyria: Lion Hunts, Siege of Lachish and Khorsabad, 710–635 BC," *The British Museum*, accessed May 2, 2022, https://www.britishmuseum.org/collection/galleries/assyria-lion-hunts.

4. Bruce K. Waltke, "*nāpash*," *Theological Wordbook of the Old Testament* (15 vols.; edited by G. Johannes Botterweck and Helmer Ringgren; translated by John T. Willis et al.; Grand Rapids, MI: Eerdmans, 1974–2006), 2:591.

5. The refrain is once more repeated in Psalm 43:5, and the close connection between the two psalms has motivated interpreters to read the two psalms as one composition, which is supported in a number of ancient Hebrew manuscripts.

6. Psalm 63 is associated with David's flight from Jerusalem when his son Absalom tried to usurp the throne. David ends up in the rock fortress of Mahanaim on the other side of the Jordan River, longing to see God's sanctuary again. Martin G. Klingbeil, "Psalms 1–75," in *Seventh-day Adventist International Bible Commentary*, ed. Jacques Doukhan, vol. 6, *Psalms, Proverbs, Ecclesiastes, Song of Songs* (Nampa, ID: Pacific Press®, 2022), 259.

7. Martin G. Klingbeil, "The Center of Gravity," *Adventist World*, July 2019, 24, 25.

8. Psalm 73 is also positioned at the seam between Book 2 (Psalms 42–72) and Book 3 (Psalms 73–89) of the psalter.

9. Dragoslava Santrac, "The Psalmists' Journey and the Sanctuary: A Study in the

Sanctuary and the Shape of the Book of Psalms," *Journal of the Adventist Theological Society* 25, no. 1 (2014): 23–42.

10. See Peter Roennfeldt, *Your Church Has Changed: Rebuilding Church and Mission Post-COVID-19* (Warburton, Australia: Signs Publishing, 2021).

11. Marty Nystrom, "As the Deer" (Universal Music—Brentwood-Benson, 1984).

12

Worship That Never Ends

The psalms were always meant to be heard and not just read. They were written to be recited in public (Psalm 118) and performed with congregational kneeling and bowing (Psalm 95). But most of all, they were meant to be sung (Psalm 96). For example, the Songs of Ascents (Psalms 120–134) were sung as pilgrims went up to Jerusalem during the annual feasts at the temple (see chapter 4). Beyond these pilgrim songs, the Hebrew root *shir*, meaning "song" or "to sing," occurs another fifty-five times in the Psalter,[1] inviting its readers and hearers to "sing a new song" (Psalm 33:3), to "sing and praise" (Psalm 21:13), or to sing "in his tent" (Psalm 27:6).

Some songs were related to specific historical situations, such as when "the Lord delivered him [David] from . . . the hand of Saul" (Psalm 18:1), or occasions like building dedications (Psalm 30 and processions to the sanctuary (Psalm 68). There are also psalms that are set to specific instruments (Psalm 4—"with stringed instruments") or have other, at times somewhat enigmatic, musical annotations (Psalm 60 "set to 'Lily of the Testimony' ").

The reconstruction of ancient Israelite music and instruments regarding the singing of the psalms is aided by archaeology (depictions of musical instruments on seals, actual instruments found, cuneiform tablets with tuning instructions, etc.). Additionally, the cantillation marks in the Hebrew Bible served to aid in the public reading and singing of the psalms in the synagogue.[2]

Beyond the music of the Bible itself, the Psalms have inspired composers and musicians throughout Christian history, creating iconic works of art that have moved listeners closer to God and His Word. George Frederic Handel became noted for his musical genius based on musical compositions of three psalms (Psalms 2; 22; and 69).[3] In the text of his most widely known oratorio, *Messiah*, the book of Psalms, after Isaiah, is the second most quoted book from the Bible. The beautiful chorus "Lift up your heads, O ye gates" (movement 33) is based on Psalm 24:7–10, a question-and-answer liturgy reminiscent of the gatekeeper questions at the temple entrance, connecting the psalm to Christ's ascension.[4]

Johann Sebastian Bach, in at least forty-seven musical works, interacted closely with the Psalms. One of his monumental passion oratorios, the St. John Passion, opens with the moving chorus "Herr, unser Herrscher" ("Lord, our Ruler"), which is a paraphrase of Psalm 8. Bach, as he often did, followed Luther's Messianic interpretation of Psalm 8 in emphasizing the paradox of Christ's glorification in the humiliation of the Cross.[5] Theology has been taught and preserved through the music of the Psalms.

Davar—Praise God from whom all blessings flow

Psalms is divided into five books, with each one ending in a doxology, a short hymn of praise to God. They vary in size, but in musical terms they seem to increase incrementally in volume, ending the psalter with a beautiful symphony of voices and instruments, praising God for His wonderful works in history against the background of the plan of salvation.

Book I (Psalms 1–41)

Blessed be the LORD God of Israel
From everlasting to everlasting!
Amen and Amen (Psalm 41:13).

Book II (Psalms 42–72)

Blessed be the LORD God, the God
  of Israel,
Who only does wondrous things!
And blessed be His glorious name
  forever!
And let the whole earth be filled
  with His glory.
Amen and Amen (Psalm 72:18, 19).

Book III (Psalms 73–89)

Blessed be the LORD forevermore!
Amen and Amen (Psalm 89:52).

Book IV (Psalms 90–106)

Blessed be the LORD God of Israel
From everlasting to everlasting!
And let all the people say, "Amen!"
  (Psalm 106:48).

Book V (Psalms 107–150)

Praise the LORD!
Praise God in His sanctuary;
Praise Him in His mighty
  firmament!
Praise Him for His mighty acts;
Praise Him according to His
  excellent greatness!
Praise Him with the sound of the
  trumpet;
Praise Him with the lute and harp!
Praise Him with the timbrel and
  dance;
Praise Him with stringed instru-
  ments and flutes!
Praise Him with loud cymbals;
Praise Him with clashing cymbals!
Let everything that has breath praise
  the LORD.
Praise the LORD! (Psalm 150).

A few interesting observations can be made about the final praises that conclude each of the five books. They are linked to each other by the Hebrew word *amen*, "amen," and these seven amens are the only occurrences of the word in the book of Psalms. They confirm (*amen* in Hebrew means "verily, truly, so be it") what each book has presented, underwriting it with the psalmist's and the congregation's praise of God.

The first doxology (Psalm 41:13) invites the congregation to bless the "LORD God of Israel," who from the beginning has manifested Himself as *Elohim* ("God"—Genesis 1:1), the God of Creation, and as *Yahweh* ("LORD"—Genesis 2:7), the God of the covenant. Both names also appear in the other doxologies, except for the doxology at the end of Book III, which directs the blessings only to *Yahweh*.

Other characteristics of God that run through the doxologies are His eternal character (Hebrew *'olam*, "everlasting, forevermore, eternal"), His unchangeability, and His everlasting claim on Israel. What we have learned about God (theology) in Book I invites a congregational response in praise (doxology).[6] The doxology at the end of Book II (Psalm 72:18, 19) draws on the same elements of God's name and His everlasting character but enhances these qualities by mentioning God's "wondrous things" (Hebrew *niphla'ot*, "wonderful deeds"), which in the Psalms (e.g., Psalm 78) usually refer to His historic acts in the plan of salvation (Creation, Exodus, patriarchs, conquest, Davidic monarchy, etc.). These parallel God's "mighty deeds" in the fifth doxology (Psalm 150:2) and serve to glorify God's "name" as expressed in His character.[7]

The third doxology at the end of Book III (Psalm 89:52) seems to dial back the volume somewhat in that it is the shortest of all five. Yet it makes a significant statement at the end of a section in the Psalms that is full of "national tragedy" (e.g., the destruction of the temple in Psalm 74 and 79) and "personal suffering"[8] (e.g., the utterly dark outlook of Psalm 88—the psalm ends in the Hebrew text with the word "darkness"). But the doxology still emphasizes the goodness of the everlasting God of Covenant (in Psalm 89 only as *Yahweh*) and underwrites all of this with a twofold Amen.

The fourth doxology (Psalm 106:48) is almost identical to the first. It ends with only one Amen, which is preceded by an invitation for all Israel to join in the amen.

Psalm 150 is the last doxology in the book of Psalms, and it connects to and contrasts with the four preceding ones. The seven amens of the four previous doxologies are answered with seven musical instruments (trumpet, lute, harp, timbrel, stringed instruments, flute, and cymbals—Psalm 150:3–5) and framed by three hallelujah shouts, one at the beginning and two at the end of the psalm (Hebrew *hallelujah*, "Praise the LORD," occurs once in Psalm 150:1 and twice in verse 6). The ten lines between these three hallelujahs all begin with an invitation to "Praise" (Hebrew *hallelu*).

One wonders if these numerical arrangements are coincidental. The number ten in the Bible can be connected to the Ten Commandments, or the "ten words" as the Decalogue is referred to in the Old Testament (Exodus 34:28; Deuteronomy 4:13; 10:4). Then there are the ten utterances of God in Creation as He speaks ten times (*wayo'mer elohim* "And God said"—Genesis 1:3, 6, 9, 11, 14, 20, 24, 26, 28, 29) to create the world and all that is within out of nothing. The number three is the number pointing to the triune Godhead (Genesis 1:1, 2, 26; Matthew 28:19; 2 Corinthians 13:14; 1 Peter 1:1, 2; etc.), complemented by the number seven, which points once more back to Creation and the Sabbath (Genesis 2:2, 3; Exodus 20:8–11; Deuteronomy 5:12–14; Leviticus 25). All of these biblically significant numbers and their arrangement remind the reader of the theological dimension of this final doxology, this final song of praise, echoing through the universe and to the end of time.

Pesher—The final praise

We get to know God by praising Him, and Psalm 150 serves as a powerful object lesson for this truth. This praise song begins with an address to Yahweh/Elohim, who resides in "His sanctuary"—a locale that is clarified in the parallel line that follows. The sanctuary of Psalm 150 appears to be the heavenly sanctuary[9] as it is in "His mighty firmament" (Genesis 1:6–8), thus opening up a cosmic, even eschatological perspective for the psalm.

Psalm 149 ends with the call to "execute on them the written judgment" (verse 9), and Psalm 150 begins with a response of praise to the one who vindicates His people. Once more, God's "mighty acts" from Creation to re-creation are recalled (Psalm 150:2) as a procession of praise moves out from the heavenly sanctuary into the cosmos. This is a scene that is reminiscent of Daniel 12:1, 2 when "Michael shall stand up" and

His "people shall be delivered, every one who is found written in the book," marking the end of the investigative judgment and the beginning of the executive judgment, when Christ returns to earth. The sequence of musical instruments corroborates this movement out of the heavenly sanctuary, as indicated by the use of the first three instruments. These cultic instruments were mainly reserved for priests and Levites within the temple (1 Chronicles 15:16; 2 Chronicles 5:12–14).

The *shofar* ("trumpet") announced religious feasts (Psalm 81:3), new kings (2 Samuel 15:10), and divine judgment (Leviticus 23:24; 25:9), while the lute and harp are specifically mentioned for accompanying temple music (2 Chronicles 5:12–14). As the procession moves out of the temple and into the courtyard, other instruments join (timbrel, stringed instruments, flutes, and cymbals), whose usage is usually associated with military victories (Exodus 15:20) and other joyful occasions (Jeremiah 31:4).

The victory procession moves further out with a joyful dance, which can be understood as prescribed cultic movements rather than a wild ecstatic dance. (The Hebrew word *makhol*, "dance," comes from the adverb "efficient, noble, worth.") Now the instruments unite with the voices of "everything that has breath," pointing once more to the cosmic dimension of the victory procession that includes all created beings—angels, humans, creatures from other worlds, and even animals.

There is one final crescendo led by "clashing cymbals," and the redeemed will enter eternity. Ancient interpreters and modern scholars have recognized the eschatological dimension of Psalm 150,[10] which goes far beyond the final doxology of the Psalter.

Edut—The great controversy ended

It was Easter Sunday sometime during the early 1980s in Pforzheim, a city in the northern Black Forest, where I grew up. When I was a teenager, my brother and I joined a semi-professional choir led by one of the leading

Lutheran church musicians in Germany.

We had just performed Bach's *St. John Passion* in front of a packed Lutheran church with about 1,200 people in the audience. Church attendance in this otherwise secular country was largely limited to Easter and Christmas. The more than two-hour-long oratorio of divinely inspired music recounting Christ's passion according to the Gospel of John ends with the final choral "Ach Herr, lass dein lieb Engelein" ("Ah, Lord, let Your dear little angel"), expressing hope in Christ's resurrection for all those who have followed Him, with a clear understanding of death as a rest and the resurrection at Christ's second advent. The music ends with a climactic assertion: "Lord Jesus Christ, hear me; I will praise you eternally!"

As the members of the choir and orchestra around me packed up their scores and instruments, I remained sitting, moved by the masterful music and its poignant message of Christ's suffering, death, and resurrection and the hope it brings us. The balcony slowly emptied, as did the church below, and finally, just the choir director, my brother, and myself remained. The director slowly walked over to us and quietly said: "I think you might be the only ones who really understood Bach's music today."

Psalm 150 gives us a glorious vision of the final moments of earth's history as Christ leaves the heavenly sanctuary and returns to earth amidst a cosmic symphony of praise, ending the great controversy in one great Hallelujah shout: "The great controversy is ended. Sin and sinners are no more. The entire universe is clean. One pulse of harmony and gladness beats through the vast creation. From Him who created all, flow life and light and gladness, throughout the realms of illimitable space. From the minutest atom to the greatest world, all things, animate and inanimate, in their unshadowed beauty and perfect joy, declare that God is love."[11]

When we lift our voices in praise to God, intimacy follows. We begin to understand and appreciate what He has done for us. Hope is renewed, and we long to be part of His eternal choir.

Tehillim—Hallelujah

Hallelujah!

For the Lord God Omnipotent reigneth.

Hallelujah!

For the Lord God omnipotent reigneth.

Hallelujah!

The kingdom of this world is become

The kingdom of our Lord, and of His Christ,

and of His Christ

And He shall reign for ever and ever

For ever and ever, for ever and ever

King of kings! and Lord of lords!

And He shall reign forever and ever

Hallelujah![12]

---

1. The total occurrences of the Hebrew root *shir* "song, to sing" in the Psalms is 71, and the following list provides a good opportunity to study the motivations, circumstances, results of singing, and the songs themselves, in the Psalms: Psalms 7:1; 13:6; 18:1; 21:13; 27:6; 28:7; 30:1; 33:3; 40:3; 42:8; 45:1; 46:1; 48:1; 57:7; 59:17; 65:1, 13; 66:1; 67:1; 68:1, 4, 26, 32, 33; 69:30; 75:1; 76:1; 83:1; 87:1, 7; 88:1; 89:1; 92:1; 96:1, 2; 98:1; 101:1; 104:33; 105:2; 106:12; 108:1, 2; 120:1; 121:1; 122:1; 123:1; 124:1; 125:1; 126:1; 127:1; 128:1; 129:1; 130:1; 131:1; 132:1; 133:1; 134:1; 137:3, 4; 138:5; 144:9; 149:1. In the rest of the Old Testament, *shir* occurs another 109 times.

2. Wynand Johannes Christian Pretorius, "Music in Ancient Israel/Palestine With Reference to Tonality and Development of the Psalms" (MA thesis, University of South Africa, 2018), https://core.ac.uk/download/pdf/196520992.pdf.

3. Charles Morris, "Handel's Messiah: Lyrics and Verse References," Haven Today Blog, Novermber, 20, 2020, https://haventoday.org/blog/handels-messiah-lyrics-verse-references/.

4. Martin G. Klingbeil, "Psalms 1–75," in *Seventh-day Adventist International Bible Commentary*, ed. Jacques Doukhan, vol. 6, *Psalms, Proverbs, Ecclesiastes, Song of Songs* (Nampa, ID: Pacific Press®, 2022), 125.

5. Daniel R. Melamed, "Focus On: Listening to Scripture in J. S. Bach's Passions,"

Oxford Biblical Studies Online, accessed August 7, 2022, https://global.oup.com/obso /focus/focus_on_listening_to_scripture. Need an account to view content.

6. Klingbeil, "Psalms 1–75," 187.

7. The doxology at the end of Book II is followed by an editorial note that the "prayers of David the son of Jesse are ended," providing an insight to the development of the psalter and pointing to earlier collections that combined Books I and II.

8. Dragoslava Santrac, "Psalms 76–150," in Doukhan, *International Bible Commentary*, 402.

9. Richard M. Davidson, "The Heavenly Sanctuary in the Old Testament," *Faculty Publications*, paper 62, Andrews University, 1970, https://digitalcommons.andrews .edu/cgi/viewcontent.cgi?article=1061&context=old-testament-pubs.

10. Gregory of Nyssa (AD 335–394), bishop in Cappadocia (modern Turkey), interpreted Psalm 150 as the "eschatological union of human and angelic worship." Graham Field, "Breaking Boundaries: The Cosmic Dimension of Worship," *Studia Patristica* 88 (2017): 83; see also Frank Lothar Hossfeld and Erich Zenger, *Psalms 3: A Commentary on Psalms 101–150*, trans. Linda M. Maloney, ed. Klaus Baltzer, *Hermeneia: A Critical and Historical Commentary on the Bible* (Minneapolis, MN: Fortress, 2011), 654–664.

11. Ellen G. White, *The Great Controversy* (Mountain View, CA: Pacific Press®, 1911), 678.

12. George Frederick Handel, "Hallelujah Chorus" (1741).

13

Wait on the Lord

This book could have ended in the previous chapter with our study of Psalm 150, the last poem in the Psalter. But wait! We're not there yet. While Michael still sits on His throne in the heavenly sanctuary, we find ourselves in a rapidly aging world that's spinning out of control toward its sad finale. How do we bridge the gap between the now and then, between the unfolding eschatology and His parousia?

Few people enjoy waiting. At the airport, the bank, the hospital, and many other public buildings, there are large spaces dedicated to the art—or agony—of waiting. There used to be piles of magazines, then TV monitors, and now, mostly, our smartphones that fill the empty spaces in our minds as we sit in the waiting room. We wait for an event to take place, a person to arrive, a plane to leave, or just our turn in the line.

I remember having to read a rather challenging theater play in high school and then attend a performance of it. Not that there was a fast-paced plot to be followed or highly philosophical dialogues to be deciphered—it was just nothingness and plainly absurd, so it seemed. In *Waiting for Godot* by Samuel Beckett, two characters (Vladimir and Estragon) meet on an otherwise empty stage next to a leafless tree. While they are waiting for Godot, although they are not sure when and where, or even if, he will show up, their conversations are trivial and their actions are meaningless. Their waiting is interrupted by Lucky, a slave, who, together with his master Pozzo joins them for a period in their nothingness and then leaves again. A boy arrives and announces that Godot will not come anymore today but tomorrow.

The second act is a slightly modified version of the first, and Godot never comes while Vladimir and Estragon never leave. Nevertheless, there is more to Godot than what my teenage mind could probably process at that time, although the utter futility was not lost on me.

There are many literary connections between the play and the Bible—beyond *Godot* and *God*—that have invited critical reflections by Christian scholars. They point to its subliminal messages of longing for community and salvation but ultimately fail to answer the existential question: Is our Christian walk just a futile and meaningless wait for an elusive God who will never come?[1]

Maybe we have completely misunderstood the biblical imperative "wait on the LORD" (Psalm 27:14) and replaced it with Beckett's existential notion of the loneliness of human existence in the absence of God and the expectation of His coming as a social construct to calm our worst fears of futility. Maybe there is a hopeful waiting that holds fast to the promises of a living God who teaches us a far more active form of waiting, a waiting filled with meaningful content and the expectation of real things to come. The book of Psalms is full of this hope, and the psalmists return to it with regularity to express what a purpose-filled "wait on the LORD" looks like from a biblical perspective.

Davar—Wait on the Lord

Waiting in Hebrew begins with the three letters *qwh*, which can be used as a verb (*qawah*, "wait") or noun (*tiqwah*, "hope"). In its different forms, the word appears twenty times in the book of Psalms, which represents almost one-quarter of the overall eighty-four occurrences in the Hebrew Old Testament. Evidently, the psalmists were enthusiastic about the concept of waiting and the hope connected with it.

While waiting in modern Western culture does not necessarily evoke positive associations, the range of meaning for *qwh* in the Psalms is outright positive: "to wait, hope, await, hope expectantly, expect, look eagerly," and as a noun, "hope, outcome, endurance, expectation"—all of which point to a connection that does not come easy to us:[2] When we are waiting, we actually are hoping, and this hope/wait has a clearly defined object—that is, God Himself. The psalmists wait for God. Notice the capitalized *You* in the book of Psalms: "On You I wait all the day" (Psalm 25:5), "My hope is in You" (Psalm 39:7), "I will wait on Your name, for it is good" (Psalm 52:9), and "For You are my hope" (Psalm 71:5). God's character as expressed through His "good" name is the guarantor for the glorious outcome of our wait, the underwriter of our hope being fulfilled. The positive outcomes for those who wait on the Lord are repeatedly enumerated by the psalmists: "Let no one who waits on You be ashamed" (Psalm 25:3), "my salvation" (verse 5), "integrity and uprightness" (verse 21), "inherit the earth/land" (Psalm 37:9, 34), "He inclined to me" (Psalm 40:1), and "You are my trust" (Psalm 71:5).

Waiting on God in the Psalms is not a passive pastime but, rather, an active pursuit of the purposes of God. The psalmist asks God to "lead me in Your truth and teach me" as he waits on God "all the day" (Psalm 25:5), reminding us of the educational character of the psalms, which are written for instruction (Psalm 60:1). Incidentally, the Hebrew word for instruction is *torah*, mostly translated as "law," which we often limit to just the Ten Commandments or the five books of Moses, the Pentateuch. As mentioned before, in a broader sense, it refers to the sum of God's instruction from Genesis to Malachi. In the New Testament, Jesus also had this fuller understanding of *torah* while quoting from Psalm 35:19

in John 15:25 and referring to the Psalms quote as being "written in their law."[3] Ultimately, as we are waiting on God, He instructs us to "Wait on the LORD, and keep His way" (Psalm 37:34), a theme that is at the heart of the Psalter and is introduced already in the first psalm, which contrasts the way of the ungodly with the way of the righteous (Psalm 1:6).[4]

These two diametrically opposed ways run through the whole book of Psalms and are also found in the final group of psalms (Psalms 146–150) known as the five hallelujah psalms (cf. Psalm 146:1, 2, 10). Waiting on the Lord is thus not idly sitting around (remember the admonition of Psalm 1:1 not to *sit* "in the seat of scoffers" [ESV]), but it means walking in the Way, following His instruction, and waiting for His will to be done in our lives.

Of course, this is not the frustrated waiting-room hope because those who wait on the Lord have a positive outlook on life and are "of good courage" (Psalm 27:14). This positive hope is extended even to the less fortunate and marginalized in society as "the hope of the poor shall not perish forever" (Psalm 9:18, ESV). The Psalter has a strong concern for the poor, and there is a group of psalms that focuses specifically on the humble, afflicted, or poor (Hebrew *'anawim*—Psalms 9; 10; 25; 34; 37; 69; 72; 109). Their waiting on the Lord, in the midst of great need, gives the rest of us who are waiting on the Lord the privilege of lightening their loads and carrying their burdens: "Bear one another's burdens, and so fulfill the law of Christ" (Galatians 6:2).

There is more. A purposeful hope and meaning-filled wait on God is not generated by ourselves; He is doing for us what we cannot do for ourselves, "for my hope is from him" (Psalm 62:5, ESV). He is the One who has "done it" (Psalm 52:9), and He will "strengthen your heart" (Psalm 27:14). Thus, God is not only the object but also the origin of our hope, and this is "most often expressed when humans are particularly aware of their finiteness and God's infiniteness (Psalm 39:4-7)."[5] The psalmists understood that our hope could be certain only as long as it is not based on human efforts but on divine provisions. Furthermore, this hope is based on the promises of God, which provide the psalmists with "an audacious certainty"[6] that considers God's future actions as something that has already been accomplished. Psalm 27:14—maybe one of the strongest exhortations in the Psalms to hope in God—is framed by the twofold command "Wait on the Lord," and in between these two admonitions, there is a confident expression of trust that "He shall strengthen your heart," which leaves no room for any doubts. Where Godot never arrives, God always comes through.

The national anthem of the modern state of Israel is called *Hatikva*, which translated means simply "the hope." It is a moving hymn based on a musical theme from Bedrich Smetana's *Moldau*. The text was written during the rise of the Zionist movement in the late 1800s, and it portrays the two-thousand-year-old hope of the Jewish people to return to the "Land of Zion and Jerusalem," which finally found its fulfillment in the formation of the State of Israel in 1948. Ultimately, our waiting on the Lord will find its last fulfillment, not in a temporary earthly state but in a re-created new earth and a heavenly Jerusalem, where all of our hopes will be met in God's presence. Until then, our hope will walk with Him along the Way.

Pesher—Lessons from a young tree

Hope and waiting are somewhat abstract concepts, and the preceding discussion has attempted to fill these concepts with more tangible meanings based on their usage in the book of Psalms. However, the etymology (the origin of words) of abstract terms in biblical Hebrew can often be traced to concrete origins.

This process began with the development of the Hebrew alphabet, which initially was pictographic: the letter *bet* (*b*) in the Paleo-Hebrew script (ב in the Hebrew square script used in most biblical manuscripts) resembles an enclosed structure, and the name of the letter (*bet*) also means "house. The Hebrew word *nepesh*, which is usually translated as "soul" in modern English versions but really refers to the "whole person," has a concrete meaning of "throat" and in this way connects to the Creation account of Genesis 2:7, where God breathes into the nostrils of the recently formed Adam, and he becomes a "living being" (*nepesh*).[7]

Another example is the Hebrew word *amen*. It usually underwrites prayers or sermons with a heartfelt "so be it" and has been incorporated untranslated into most modern languages. The Hebrew root word *'mn* is usually rendered as the abstract concept of "faithfulness, reliability, steadfastness," while its concrete etymology can be connected to a "pillar" or "doorpost" (thus equaling the abstract concept of *stability*)—or even to a guardian or "wet nurse" (Hebrew *'omen*—see Numbers 11:12; 2 Kings 10:1, 5; Isaiah 49:23; 60:4; Ruth 4:16; Esther 2:7, 20; Lamentations 4:5), locating it in the realm of childrearing (thus equaling the abstract concepts of *faithfulness, care,* and *constant support*).[8] These concrete etymologies can often shed light on the abstract concepts.

The etymology of *qwh*, "wait, hope," can be linked to the noun *qaw*, "measuring line, cord, rope," and an alternative translation for the verb *qawah* is "gather together" (Genesis 1:9). In Joshua 2:18 and 21, Rahab ties a red cord into her window—the only time in the Old Testament that the Hebrew word *tiqwah* is translated as "cord, rope" and not as "hope"— thus saving her family and herself when Jericho falls. This may be what hope is: tying ourselves with a rope to the life-giving promises of God like a young tree is bound to a supporting post to provide support and stability. In recognizing our own lack of strength, we connect ourselves to the Source of all power. It is interesting to note that in several verses, the undoing of our hope is connected to the Hebrew verb *karat*, "to cut off"—when we lose hope, the cord between God and us is cut off: "Surely there is a future, and your hope will not be cut off" (Proverbs 23:18, ESV; see also Proverbs 24:14; Ezekiel 37:11).

Edut—Perseverance

I enjoy running. Long distances. For the past twelve years, I have participated in the 7 Bridges Marathon in Chattanooga, Tennessee. The 26.2-mile (42.195-kilometer) course crosses the Tennessee River seven times (hence the name), and I generally enjoy the first twenty miles. After that, the enjoyment slowly gives way to aching legs and low energy levels, which coincide with an often-lonely stretch along the beautiful river, as the runners have somewhat thinned out by that time. This is the time when I hope to soon see my wife Thandi, who has run the 4 Bridges Marathon, the corresponding half marathon version of the race. By the time I approach the end of the race, she has long crossed the finish line and, after resting a bit, has returned to meet me at about mile 24.5.

I hope and "wait for Thandi." The moment I can connect my waning energy to her recovered one, I know that she will see me through the final stretch. She encourages me, cheers me on, and gives me water and maybe an energy gel. And before I know it, I turn the corner and see the finish line. Together we have persevered, something the psalmists already understood three thousand years ago: "The psalmists found the secret of 'waiting on the Lord' as they fixed their eyes on Him and bound their feebleness to His strength, leaning on the everlasting arms (Deut. 33:27)."[9]

Paul uses the same metaphor of running in a number of places throughout his writings, and in Hebrews 6:19, 20, he connects it to a hope (Greek *elpis*), a forerunner, and a rope that holds us firmly: "This *hope* we have as an anchor of the soul, both sure and steadfast, and which enters the Presence behind the veil, where the forerunner has entered for us, even Jesus, having become High Priest forever according to the order of Melchizedek." Here, Paul clearly values the Old Testament idea of hope as a tangible commodity based on the historical realities of Christ's high priestly ministry. As we connect our feeble strength to the anchor rope that reaches behind the curtain, we follow our forerunner, who will pull us into the very presence of God.[10]

Tehillim—Hope is a rope

Hope is a rope
Hung in a window
Crimson red
A house on Jericho's wall
And then she waits
Rahab with her family
Until they come
Silently marching around the city
God's presence with them
Silently until the seventh day
And the seventh time
Trumpets sound, people shout
Mighty walls fall
Except the house on the wall
With the crimson rope
Hung in the window
Rahab lives
Messiah's line
Our hope, still crimson red
His blood shed on Calvary
Gives hope, like a rope
To reach eternity.
    —Martin G. Klingbeil

---

1. Samuel Terrien, "A Theological Look at *Waiting for Godot*," *Theology Today* 46, no. 2 (1989):139–153.

2. Daniel Schibler, "הוק (# 7747)," in *New International Dictionary of Old Testament*

Theology & Exegesis, ed. Willem A. VanGemeren, 5 vols. (Grand Rapids, MI: Zondervan, 1997), 3:892, 893.

3. There are a number of other places in the New Testament that point to this more comprehensive understanding of *torah* (or *nomos* in Greek), e.g., John 10:34; 12:34; and 1 Corinthians 14:21.

4. Martin G. Klingbeil, "Psalms 1–75," in *Seventh-day Adventist International Bible Commentary,* ed. Jacques Doukhan, vol. 6, *Psalms, Proverbs, Ecclesiastes, Song of Songs* (Nampa, ID: Pacific Press®, 2022), 44–47; Ary A. Roest Crollius, "*DeReK* in the Psalms," *Biblical Theology Bulletin* 4, no. 3 (1974): 312–317, https://doi.org/10.1177/014610797400400303.

5. Schibler, "הוק (# 7747)," in VanGemeren, *New International Dictionary,* 3:894.

6. Schibler, 895.

7. Klingbeil, "Psalms 1–75," 80n3.

8. Deena Aranoff, "The Biblical Root *'mn*: Retrieval of a Term and its Household Context," in *Mothers in the Jewish Cultural Imagination,* ed. Marjorie Lehman, Jane L. Kanarek, and Simon J. Bronner, Jewish Cultural Studies, vol. 5 (Liverpool: Littman Library of Jewish Civilization and Liverpool University Press, 2017), 327–341.

9. Martin G. Klingbeil, "Perseverance /pərsəˈvɪrəns/," *Adventist World,* May 1, 2021, 10, 11.

10. William G. Johnsson, "Hebrews," in *Andrews Bible Commentary. Light. Depth. Truth.,* ed. Ángel Manuel Rodríguez (Berrien Springs, MI: Andrews University Press, 2022), 2:1836.